Workbook

MORE! 3

Gerngross · Puchta · Holzmann
Stranks · Lewis-Jones

Enriched course

HELBLING LANGUAGES

Liebe Schülerin, liebe Schüler!

Neben vielen Übungen, mit Hilfe derer du deine Kenntnisse der englischen Sprache erweitern und festigen kannst, findest du im Workbook am Ende jeder Unit auch eine Auflistung des Lernvokabulars, also der wichtigsten Wörter und Phrasen aus der jeweiligen Unit.

Diese Wortlisten sind in drei Abschnitte unterteilt:

1. Word file

Unter dieser Überschrift werden jene Wörter und Ausdrücke nochmals aufgelistet, die im mit Vocabulary bezeichneten Abschnitt einer Unit im Student's Book eingeführt und in den darauf folgenden Aktivitäten geübt werden.

2. MORE Words and phrases

In diesem Abschnitt findest du die wichtigsten Wörter aus der jeweiligen Unit im Student's Book. Sie sind in der Reihenfolge aufgelistet, wie sie im Student's Book vorkommen, und zur leichteren Orientierung auch mit der jeweiligen Nummer einer Aktivität aus dem Student's Book gekennzeichnet: 1, 2 usw.

Wichtig: Jene Wörter und Wortgruppen, die fett gedruckt sind, kommen im Alltag ganz häufig vor. Du solltest sie wirklich im Schlaf auswending können!

Zusatzinformation: Der Vollständigkeit halber soll auch noch darauf hingewiesen werden, dass es natürlich viele andere Wörter gibt, die im Student's Book eingeführt werden, die aber im Lernvokabular im Workbook nicht vorkommen. Der Grund dafür ist, dass sie im Alltag nicht so häufig gebraucht werden und daher nicht zum eigentlichen Lernvokabular gehören. Du findest sie alle – alphabetisch gereiht – in der Nachschlagliste am Ende deines Student's Book. Mit Hilfe dieser Liste kannst du schnell die Bedeutung neu vorgekommenen Wörter nachschlagen.

Noch ein Tipp!

Wer eine Sprache gut beherrschen möchte, sollte darauf achten, das sein Wortschatz ständig wächst. Das heißt aber auch, dass man schon gelernte Wörter regelmäßig wiederholen muss. Geh deshalb immer wieder die Wortlisten am Ende der Units in den Workbooks der 1. und 2. Klasse durch – du solltest dir davon möglichst alle gut merken!

Mit Bescheid vom 4. Oktober 2007, GZ: BMUKK-5.000/52-V/9/2006, hat das Bundesministerium für Unterricht, Kunst und Kultur das Unterrichtsmittel „MORE! Workbook 3" von Gerngross u.a. antragsgemäß in der vorliegenden Fassung gemäß §14 Abs. 2 und 5 des Schulunterrichtsgesetzes, BGBl. Nr. 472/86 und gemäß den derzeit geltenden Lehrplänen als für den Unterrichtsgebrauch an Hauptschulen und an allgemein bildenden höheren Schulen für die Klasse 3 im Unterrichtsgegenstand Englisch (1. lebende Fremdsprache) geeignet erklärt.

MORE! WORKBOOK 3
by Günter Gerngross, Herbert Puchta, Christian Holzmann, Jeff Stranks, Peter Lewis-Jones

Design and layout by Amanda Hockin
Illustrated by Svjetlan Junaković, Roberto Battestini, Francesca Carabelli, Sergio Raul Cingolati, Björn Pertoft, Giovanni Rolandi, Lorenzo Sabbatini.

Printed by Athesia

First published 2008

ISBN 978-3-85272-097-5

Schulbuchnummer: 140.675

www.helblinglanguages.at

Contents

Zeichenerklärung

● leichte Aufgabenstellung

■ Aufgabenstellung mittleren Schwierigkeitsgrades

★ anspruchsvolle Aufgabenstellung

▶ SB p. 15 Diese Übungen passen zur angegebenen Seite im Student's Book.

UNIT 1 The greatest band ever

Revision Vocabulary

1 One word in each list doesn't belong. Mark it with a cross.

	a)	b)	c)	d)	e)
1	☐ Maths	☐ PE	☐ Geography	☒ village	☐ Art
2	☐ wardrobe	☐ ghost	☐ vampire	☐ witch	☐ pumpkin
3	☐ hotel	☐ chemist's	☐ bank	☐ olive	☐ railway station
4	☐ cage	☐ hill	☐ fields	☐ lake	☐ beach
5	☐ plums	☐ grapes	☐ cabbage	☐ fog	☐ peppers
6	☐ uncle	☐ lamp	☐ cousin	☐ aunt	☐ grandfather
7	☐ cooker	☐ bungalow	☐ armchair	☐ sink	☐ radiator
8	☐ stroke	☐ wash up	☐ brush	☐ feed	☐ walk
9	☐ town	☐ surfing	☐ tennis	☐ basketball	☐ skiing
10	☐ snow	☐ fog	☐ showers	☐ thunderstorm	☐ rug

2 Match the lists in 1 with the titles below.

- ☐ Family members
- ☐ School subjects
- ☐ Food
- ☐ Furniture
- ☐ Halloween
- ☐ Looking after pets
- ☐ Weather
- ☐ Natural places
- ☐ Places in a town
- ☐ Sports

3 Which words in 1 can you find in the picture? Tick the words in 1.

4 Add two words to each list in 1.

END OF REVISION SECTION

5 Complete the crossword. The secret word is one of the Beatles' most famous songs. What is it?

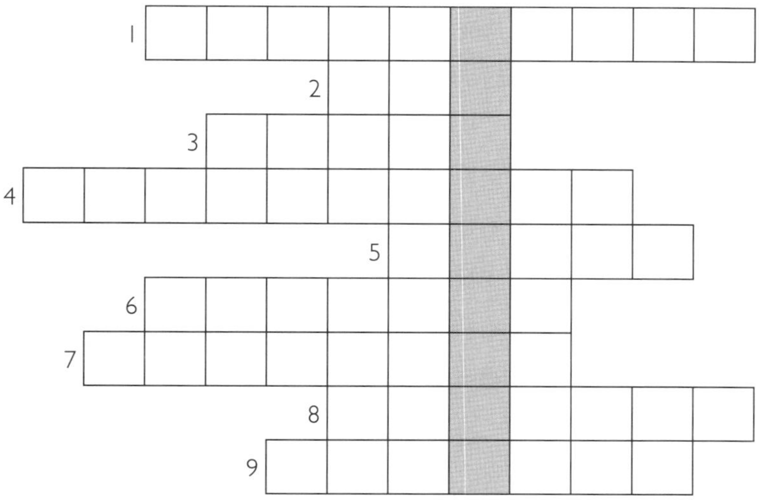

1 John Lennon played with this band before he started the Beatles.
2 Thirty years after the band finished, this CD showed how popular they still are.
3 Ringo played this instrument.
4 The band played their first American show in this city.
5 This part of the body was in the title of their eighth album.
6 The band spent their early years playing in this German city.
7 The song that started it all.
8 The man who made it impossible for the Beatles to play together again.
9 Lennon was living here when he died.

6 Write the year when:

1 Paul McCartney was born. ....
2 the *Fab Four* first played together. ....
3 the band was at the top of the American charts for a long time. ....
4 the band released perhaps their greatest album. ....
5 complaints stopped the band's final show. ....
6 *One* was number one in the charts all over the world. ....

7 Read the dialogue between the critic Paul Sacks and a singer on *Superstars*. Complete with the words in the box.

give up
way
give
training
get
audition
make
takes

Sacks Simon, Simon. Let me stop you there.
Simon What, already? I've only just started.
Sacks I don't need to hear any more. That was probably the worst [1]................................. I've ever had to listen to.
Simon Oh, come on. I wasn't that bad.
Sacks Simon, yes you were. I don't know where you got the idea you could sing, but you really have to [2]................................. that dream now.
Simon It was my mum. She says I have a lovely voice and that I have what it [3]................................. to be a famous singer. She told me I should [4]................................. this show a try.
Sacks Well, she doesn't know anything. Simon, you are not going to [5]................................. it in this job. I promise you.
Simon Maybe when I've had a bit more [6]................................. .
Sacks No. Not with all the help in the world.
Simon Well, I think you're wrong. I know I'm on the [7]................................. up and nothing you can say is going to stop that.
Sacks Well, good luck and [8]................................. back to me when you have your first number one.
Simon I will. You'll see. You'll be sorry one day.

▶ SB pp. **6, 7, 8, 9**

8 Complete the dialogues with the interviewer's questions.

~~What's your favourite band, Nigel?~~
What about the words they sing?
Do you like dancing, Janice?
Do you ever download it off the internet?
And where do you get your music from?
What do you like about them?
What kind of songs do you like dancing to?
But do you have a favourite band to dance to?
Do you listen to a lot of music, Henry?

1 **Interviewer** What's your favourite band, Nigel?
Nigel That's a difficult question. *Maroon 5*, I think.
Interviewer ....
Nigel Well, their songs have always got good melodies.
Interviewer ....
Nigel Yeah, their lyrics aren't bad, but their music is better.

2 **Interviewer** ....
Janice Yes, I love it.
Interviewer ....
Janice Anything that's got a good rhythm.
Interviewer ....
Janice At the moment it's the *Pussycat Dolls*. They're great to dance to.

3 **Interviewer** ....
Henry Yeah, I listen to at least one CD every day.
Interviewer ....
Henry Well, I probably buy two CDs a month and I borrow some of my friends'.
Interviewer ....
Henry No, I like to buy CDs better.

9 Write your answers to the interviewer's questions.

1 What song do you like best?
....

2 What well-known song do you hate most in the world?
....

3 Do you like dancing?
....

4 Where do you get your music from?
....

5 What's your favourite band?
....

6 Tell us about a song that is special for you.
....
....

7 Where do you like listening to music?
....

8 What's the most important thing in a song for you?
....
....

▶ SB p. 9

★ **10** **Read the text about *The Band*. Are the sentences true or false?**

Some great bands, like *The Beatles,* always stay popular, but some bands people forget. *The Band*, from the same time as the Beatles, are a good example. They started as *Ronnie Hawkins & the Hawks* and for four years, from 1959 to 1963, were one of the hottest rock'n'roll bands in America. Ronnie Hawkins was a difficult man and he left the group in 1963. However, the rest of the group chose a new name: *The Band*. In 1966 they met up with Bob Dylan and he invited them to be his backing band on tour.

In 1968, *The Band* released their first album *Music From Big Pink*. There was a typical sound to *The Band*: you could hear five individual voices and instruments mixing folk, blues, gospel, R&B, classical and rock'n'roll. Their breakthrough* album was *The Band* in 1969 and they suddenly became really famous. Their next albums were all very popular. In 1974, they went on tour with Bob Dylan. Many people said they were better than Dylan himself. In 1976, they released a *Best of ...* -album, and it all finished with *The Last Waltz*, the soundtrack for the film about *The Band* by Martin Scorcese (1978). The film shows their farewell concert from 1976 and also famous musicians like Bob Dylan, Van Morrison, Joni Mitchell and Eric Clapton.

They got back together a few times in the 90s but never with their songwriter and guitarist, Robbie Robertson. These days, most people have forgotten about them. However, many rock critics say that *The Band* are one of the most important groups in the history of rock'n'roll.

VOCABULARY
***breakthrough** – Durchbruch

	T	F
1 *The Band* started in 1958.	☐	☐
2 Ronnie Hawkins was a member of *The Band*.	☐	☐
3 *The Band's* music was a mixture of different styles.	☐	☐
4 *The Band* was the album that made them really famous.	☐	☐
5 They only went on tour with Dylan once.	☐	☐
6 *The Band* split up in 1976.	☐	☐
7 Some of *The Band* got back together in the 1990's.	☐	☐
8 Many music fans agree that *The Band* played an important part in making popular music what it is today.	☐	☐

★ **11** **Research a band or a pop group on the Internet. Write a brief informative text and say what you think of them.**

▶ SB p. 10

Grammar Present and past simple revision

● **12** **Complete the text with the words in the box.**

Shannon Green is lead guitar player with *The Sweet Lemons*. We caught up with her on tour to ask a few questions.

plays
does
do
sings
don't
doesn't
writes
play
write
sing

Interviewer Tell us a bit about the band.

Shannon Well, there are four of us. Dan and I [1]............................ the guitar. Bradley [2]............................ and plays bass and Kevin [3]............................ the drums.

Interviewer Do you [4]............................ ?

Shannon I sometimes sing backing vocals, but that's all.

Interviewer What kind of music [5]............................ the band play?

Shannon Pop and a bit of rock.

Interviewer And [6]............................ you write your own music?

Shannon Well, Bradley [7]............................ all the lyrics and we all [8]............................ the music.

Interviewer And do you play other band's songs?

Shannon No, we [9]......................... Bradley [10]......................... like playing other people's music.

■ **13** **Read the text about how Shannon joined *The Sweet Lemons* and put the verbs into the *past tense* to complete it.**

Shannon ......dreamt...... (dream) of being a pop star, so she was very happy when she [1]............................ (get) an electric guitar for her 13th birthday. There was only one problem. She [2]................................ (not know) how to play it. She [3]............................ (take) some lessons and [4]................................ (practise) every afternoon after school. After six months she was very good. But Shannon [5]................................ (not want) to play on her own. She [6]............................ (want) to play in a band. There was one band at her school, *The Sweet Lemons* but they all [7]............................ (study) in year six. They were all 15 and Shannon [8]................................ (not think) they would want her.

At the end of the school year, there was a party. *The Sweet Lemons* wanted to play at the party. But the day before the show, the guitar player, Dan, [9]............................ (fall) ill. The doctor [10]............................ (say) he had to stay in bed for a week. What [11]............................ (can) they do? They [12]............................ (can not) play without their guitarist.

Shannon [13]............................ (have) an idea. She [14]............................ (go) up to the band and [15]............................ (talk) to them. The band leader Bradley was interested. Shannon played her guitar and the band thought she was very good. Bradley [16]............................ (ask) her to play for them at the show. The show was a great hit and all the kids [17]............................ (love) the band. Everybody [18]............................ (agree) that Shannon was very good.

So what happened when Dan got better? There was only one way to keep everyone happy. *The Sweet Lemons* now have two guitarists.

▶ SB p. 11

Word File

He/She's going to **make it**.

give sth **a try**

You have(n't) got **what it takes**.

She's got a **good voice**.

We'll **get back** to you.

Don't **give up!**

He/She's **on the way** up.

MORE Words and Phrases

●	1	album	*The greatest Beatles' album was "Sergeant Pepper's Lonely Hearts Club Band".*	Album
		appearance	*With "Love me do" they made their first appearance in the UK charts.*	Erscheinen; Auftritt
		compilation	*The album "One" is a compilation of all their number one hits.*	Sammlung
		cover	*The album's cover showed pictures of many of the band's idols.*	Abdeckung; hier: Cover
		death	*John Lennon's death was a great shock.*	Tod
		performance	*The band's performance was a big success.*	Vorführung
		reach	*The album reached number one in the charts.*	erreichen
		record		(Schall)platte
		release	*She released her first solo album in 2003.*	freilassen, hier: veröffentlichen
		rhythm	*They danced to the rhythym of the song.*	Rhythmus, Takt
		vocals	*Is that John Lennon on vocals?*	Gesang
★	7	**brave**	*You have to be brave to sing on Superstar.*	mutig, unerschrocken
		maybe	*Maybe you'll win.*	vielleicht, möglicherweise
●	8	tune	*I like songs with a good tune.*	Melodie
★	10	**by** (Robbie Williams)	*The song "Angels" is sung by Robbie Williams.*	von (Robbie Williams)
		dance floor	*When I like a song, I get up on the dance floor.*	Tanzfläche
		for a **few** minutes	*And I dance for a few minutes.*	einige Minuten lang
		lyrics	*I like songs with a good tune. I don't care about the lyrics.*	
		well-known	*She's a well-known star.*	(allgemein) bekannt; berühmt
★	11	I can't **stand** something	*Do you like Robbie Williams? I can't stand his music.*	etwas nicht leiden können
		I don't **mind.**	*Of course you can go. I don't mind.*	Ich habe nichts dagegen.
		melody	*This song has a great melody.*	Melodie
★	13	award	*Who won the Songwriter of the Year Award?*	Preis, Auszeichnung
		several	*Beyoncé starred in several films.*	einige, verschiedene

UNIT 2 What a coincidence!

Revision Vocabulary

● 1 **Complete the song titles with the words in the box.**

make
way
give
up
takes
back

1 'Don't give .... on me baby.'

2 'I'm going to .... it to the top.'

3 'You've got what it .... for me.'

4 'Can't we .... it one more try.'

5 'I'll get .... to you in the morning.'

6 'I'm on the .... up.'

■ 2 **Which of the song titles in 1 means:**

a I'll tell you my answer tomorrow. ☐
b I'm going to be a star. ☐
c Stay with me. ☐
d I'm becoming famous. ☐
e You're everything I need. ☐
f Give me another chance. ☐

Grammar Present simple and past simple

■ 3 **Complete the text with the correct form of the verb in brackets. Use the present simple or the past simple.**

I just ....*love*.... (love) Robbie Williams. Nobody 1.......................... (sing) as well as him, nobody 2.......................... (dance) as well as him. He's the best. He 3.......................... (not be) scared to do things differently. He 4.......................... (not care) what people think of him.

I first 5.......................... (fall) in love with Robbie when he 6.......................... (sing) in the boy band *Take That*. I 7.......................... really 8.......................... (not like) the other members of the band. They were boring. But Robbie … well he was always different. When he 9.......................... (leave) the band, I 10.......................... (not be) sad. I 11.......................... (know) he would be an even bigger star on his own. And I was right.

Of course I 12.......................... (have got) all his CDs and DVDs. I 13.......................... (spend) most my money on buying his music. I also 14.......................... (go) to his shows when he 15.......................... (play) in London. The first show I 16.......................... (go) to was at Wembley Arena in 1998. My dad 17.......................... (buy) me tickets for my birthday present. But he 18.......................... (not buy) just any tickets – they were for the front row. It 19.......................... (be) fantastic. Robbie 20.......................... (look) at me all the time. I 21.......................... (love) my dad almost as much as I love Robbie.

END OF REVISION SECTION

4 Choose the correct words. Write.

On Christmas day twin sisters Levinia and Lorraine [1]............................ (left/got) their houses and [2]............................ (found/got) into their cars. Lorraine [3]............................ (wanted/heard) to take a Christmas present to Levinia's house and Levinia wanted to take a present to Lorraine's house. But the sisters [4]............................ (came/ended up) in hospital because they had an [5]............................ (present/accident) on an icy country road. The twins crashed into each other's cars.

"Twins sometimes do the same [6]............................ (things/problems) at the same time," said their mother. "It's a coincidence that they crashed into each other's car. But it's really [7]............................ (strange/nice) that it happened on Christmas day!"

"We thought it was a joke," police said. "We really couldn't [8]............................ (think/believe) it was true. The twin sisters crashed into each other's cars on Christmas day and [9]............................ (your/their) names are – Lorraine and Levinia Christmas!"

5 Match the sentence halves.

1 The twins wanted to take	☐	Levinia Christmas.
2 But they ended up	☐	happened on Christmas day.
3 They crashed into	1	presents to each other's houses.
4 It was very strange that it	☐	in hospital.
5 Their names are Lorraine and	☐	each other's cars.

6 Read the *Christmas accident coincidence* story in your Student's Books (p. 12) again. Can you find five mistakes in the summary?

THE HERALD WEDNESDAY DEC 28TH

Sisters in Coincidence Crash

Sisters Lorraine and Levinia were lucky yesterday when their cars crashed into each other in the city centre. The sisters were on their way to a party at their mother's house when a dog ran onto the road. Lorraine is a year older than Levinia, but she lost control of her car and crashed into her sister coming the other way. Luckily neither sister was hurt.

7 Write numbers. Which of these objects can you:

1 listen to?
2 talk on?
3 try on?
4 pay?

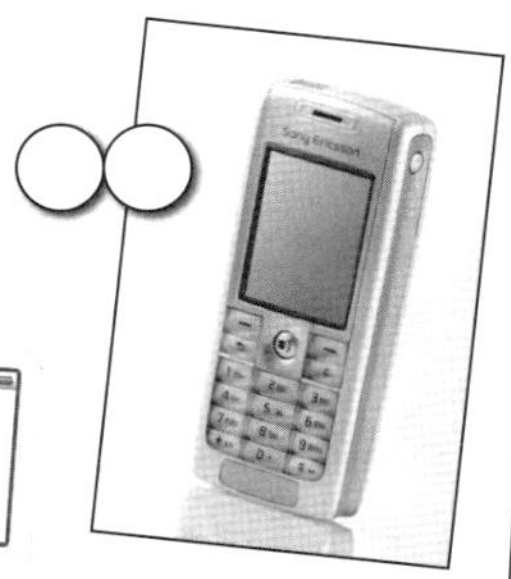

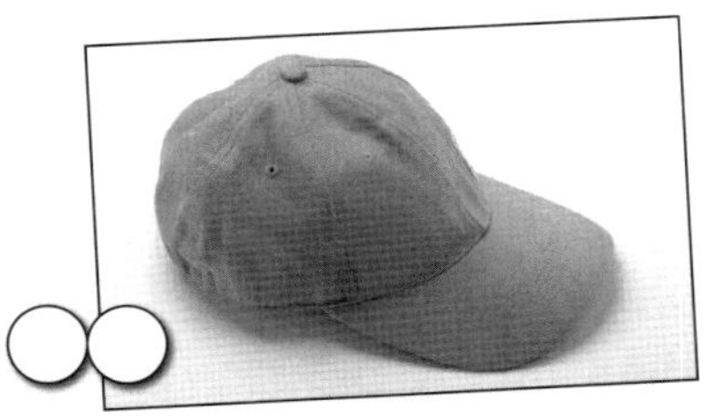

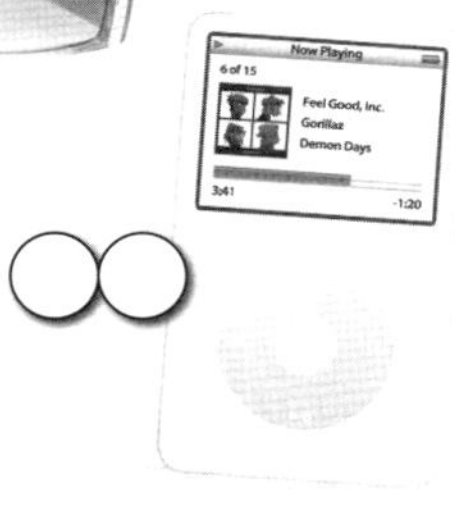

8 Use the verbs to write sentences about the objects above.

They were so angry that they left the restaurant without paying the bill.

SB p. 12

★ **9** **Read the story *Talking to Belinda* in your Student's Books (p.14/15) again and decide:**

a) who said each of these sentences.
b) the order they said them in the story.

		order
1	.... said 'I'm going to take a year out around Europe. I'm so excited.'	☐
2	.... said 'Mr Cooper, you really have to stop phoning me every night. I've got work to do.'	☐
3	.... said 'You're busy tonight Stan. Have you got a table for me?'	☐
4	The waiter said 'Would you like a table next to the window, madam?'	1
5	.... said 'Oh no. I've left her number on the subway.'	☐
6	.... said 'Belinda lived here until about two months ago.'	☐
7	.... said 'Can I invite you out to dinner some day soon?'	☐
8	.... said 'Do you remember that girl I was talking to? Do you know who she is?'	☐
9	.... said 'It's one of my favourite books. In fact this is the fifth time that I've read it.'	☐
10	.... said 'Hello, is that Belinda?'	☐

■ **10** **Are you like these two people? Do you think the same? Tick each of the sentences that are true for you, too, and then add up the totals.**

1. I like bright colours. ○
2. I have lots of friends, but only a few who are really important to me. ○
3. I'm really interested in ghosts and things like that. ○
4. I never do my homework on time. ○
5. My perfect holiday would be skiing in the Alps. ○
6. I'm not really interested in politics. ○
7. School holidays are too long. ○
8. I want to live in a different country when I'm older. ○
9. I hate computers. ○
10. Wednesday is the best day of the week. ○

total

1. I've got no idea what I want to be when I'm older. ○
2. I'm worried about the future of our earth. ○
3. I couldn't live with out loud music. ○
4. The mornings are the best part of the day. ○
5. I love maths. ○
6. I love to get up late at the weekends. ○
7. I need more holidays. ○
8. I talk too much on the phone. ○
9. There's more to life than money. ○
10. You never have to say sorry to a true friend. ○

total

★ **11** **Which of these two people would you like to meet most? Write a paragraph and say why.**

▶ SB pp. 14, 15, 16

★ **12** **Read the story and choose the best title for it.**

- ☐ The helpful strangers
- ☐ A lucky coincidence
- ☐ That's what friends are for
- ☐ A really bad holiday

The Grangers were on holiday in one of the wilder parts of Scotland, very much in the north. It was their first holiday in Scotland and they rented* a small house, nearly an hour's drive away from Braemar. 'Lovely walks,' Mr Granger said. 'Good for birdwatching, too.' And when it rained and rained for the first two days they were there, he said, 'A bit of rain is quite okay. It's good for the roses.' And he laughed at his own joke, because there were, of course, no roses.

One day they drove into Braemar to do some shopping. After shopping, they went for some tea and cake. They were sitting in a nice corner of the café, enjoying their third cup, when suddenly Mr Granger whispered to his wife: 'Don't look. It's the Warners.' Mr Warner worked with Mr Granger, but he didn't like him much. 'I wonder how they got here. They usually go on holiday to France. Bert keeps telling me that everything is so interesting there.'

Mr Granger quickly tried to hide behind his newspaper, but it was too late.
'Oh hello, Nick,' Bert Warner shouted. 'Now that's what I call a coincidence. Right in the middle of Braemar and who do I meet – good old Nick.' 'Oh hello, what a nice surprise,' Mr Granger said. 'What bad luck!' he thought.

The Grangers and the Warners spent another half hour together. 'You must come and see us,' Mr Warner said. 'We've rented a small house right here in Braemar. Here's my mobile phone number.' 'Glad to,' Mr Granger said. 'No way,' he said to his wife as soon as the Warners left.

Two days later Mr Granger had an accident when he was walking through a wood. His wife had to phone an ambulance. They had to break off their holidays and go home, but Mrs Granger couldn't drive. What could she do? Then she remembered the Warners. She phoned them. They were only too happy to help. Bert picked Nick up from hospital and he drove the Grangers down to Canterbury where they lived. Gladys Warner drove down their own car so they could go back to enjoy the nine days left of their holiday. They took Gladys' brother with them. He didn't know where to go on holiday and was happy to rent the small house for a week and pay the Grangers the rent money.

VOCABULARY
***rent** – mieten

■ **13** **Read the story again and tick the boxes T (*True*) or F (*False*).**

		T	F
1	The Grangers often spent their holidays in Scotland.	☐	☐
2	They had bad weather at the beginning of the holiday.	☐	☐
3	Mr Granger and Mr Warner worked together.	☐	☐
4	Mr Granger didn't really want to talk to Mr Warner.	☐	☐
5	The Warners had rented a small house just down the road from the Grangers.	☐	☐
6	Mr Granger had a bad accident climbing a mountain.	☐	☐
7	Mrs Granger stayed in Scotland to wait for her husband.	☐	☐
8	The Grangers lost money because they had to pay for a week in the small house when they weren't there.	☐	☐

★ **14** **Write either:**

1 A thank you letter from Mr Granger to Mr Warner.
2 A postcard from Mr Warner to Mr Granger at the end of his holiday.

▶ SB p. 17

GRAMMAR Past continuous

■ **15 Find seven verbs in the correct form to complete the sentences. (←→↑↓)**

W	O	R	K	I	N	G	Z
A	R	E	A	D	I	N	G
T	F	P	O	P	L	A	D
C	E	E	E	L	L	R	E
H	L	I	O	I	E	E	P
I	L	A	T	E	F	A	A
N	W	O	R	Y	A	D	C
G	N	I	T	A	E	F	S
S	T	A	R	T	E	D	E

1 I was ......watching...... TV when the phone rang
2 We were playing tennis when it .... to rain.
3 When the ball broke the window, we were .... breakfast.
4 When the lights went out, I was .... at the computer.
5 She was dancing when she .... over.
6 When the alarm clock .... , I was having a bath.
7 Bob was .... a book when there was a knock at the door.

★ **16 Put the verb in brackets in the past simple or past continuous and complete the story.**

I ...was walking.. (walk) down the road when I [1]................................ (see) a wallet on the ground. I [2]................................ (open) it and [3]................................ (find) a £10 note in it. There was nothing else, no name, no address, no credit cards – nothing. I [4]................................ (think) about what to do when I [5]................................ (see) my friend Daisy. She [6]................................ (shop) but she [7]................................ (not look) very happy. I [8]................................ (ask) her what was wrong. She really wanted to buy a beautiful handbag for her mum's birthday. It was £20 but she only had £10. Then I [9]................................ (know) what to do with the money from the wallet.

■ **17 Use the pictures and words to write sentences.**

1

break leg / play football
Dawn broke her leg when she was playing football.

2

drink coffee / drop cup
Henry ....
....
....

3

walk dog / start raining
June ....
....
....

4

work at the computer / chair break
Viv ....
....
....

5

read a book / headache start
Miriam ....
....
....

6

listen to MP3 player / crash into a lamp post.
Billy ....
....
....

7

fall asleep / teacher talk
Sue ....
....
....

8

eat apple / tooth fall out
Richard ....
....
....

▶ SB pp. 13, 19

Everyday English The mystery boy

Look at the phrases on p. 18 in your Student's Book again. Use them to complete the dialogues.

1 **Teacher:** OK, four of you didn't do the homework. So you'll all get more homework for tomorrow.

Student: .... Most of us did their homework alright, why should we do more?

2 **Sally** Hey, Gerry – .... ! There's a motorbike coming!

Gerry Phew! That was close. I didn't hear it as I had my earphones on.

3 **Peter** It seems nobody wants me in their team.

John .... Last time we played, you never passed the ball to anyone.

4 **Lucy** I just can't concentrate when everyone is so noisy.

Anna .... I find it difficult to work here, too.

MORE Words and Phrases

●	1	coincidence	*It's a coincidence they crashed into each other's car.*	Zufall; Glück, Fügung
		What a ...!	*What a coincidence! We crashed into each other.*	Was für ein ...!
		icy	*The roads are very icy in winter.*	vereist
		take sth somewhere	*They were taking presents to each other's houses.*	etwas irgendwohin bringen
■	3	among	*I found your message among my emails.*	unter
		belong to	*The book belongs to me. It's mine.*	gehören
		daily	*We bring you this programme daily.*	täglich
		incredible	*That story is incredible.*	unglaublich
		someone else	*Does this book belong to you or to someone else?*	jemand anders
		suitcase	*I lost my suitcase at the airport.*	Koffer
●	5	**bill**	*Let me pay the bill.*	Rechnung
		sunglasses (pl)	*When the sun is strong, wear sunglasses.*	Sonnenbrille
		try on	*I tried on a hat at the shop.*	anprobieren
■	7	careless	*You've lost my mobile phone? How careless of you!*	unvorsichtig, leichtsinnig
		handbag	*She has a handbag over her shoulder.*	Handtasche
		I beg your pardon.	*I beg your pardon, do you know where the station is?*	Entschuldigung, tut mir leid
■	8	dial	*Make sure you dial the telephone number correctly.*	wählen
		have an **interest** in sth	*She has a great interest in classical music.*	sich für etwas interessieren
		I'm sorry.	*I didn't mean to interrupt. I'm sorry.*	Das tut mir leid.
		I'm sorry?	*I'm sorry? I didn't hear what you were saying.*	Wie bitte?
		interrupt	*Let me finish. Please don't interrupt.*	Unterbrechen
		meal	*I had my favourite meal last night. Pizza!*	Mahlzeit, Essen
		move out (of)	*She moved out of her flat last week.*	ausziehen (aus)
		over there	*Can you see that car over there?*	dort drüben
		wave	*The waves were very high in the storm last night.*	Welle
		who	*She's the one who called you.*	der/die/das
★	9	**not any more**	*Belinda doesn't live here any more.*	nicht mehr
		surprised	*He was surprised to see her name in the book.*	überrascht
■	10	**decide**	*Decide what happens next.*	(sich) entscheiden
★	11	fall in love	*They met in Paris and fell in love.*	sich verlieben
■	13	**Me too.**	*Me, too! What a coincidence.*	Ich auch.
	DI	pavement	*Watch out with that ball! This is a pavement!*	Gehsteig, Bürgersteig

▶ SB p. 18

UNIT 3 Going on a journey

Revision Vocabulary

● **1 Look at the picture and write sentences using one word from box A and one word from box B each time.**

Box A	Box B
pay	sunglasses
listen to	MP3 player
talk	~~lemonade~~
try on	ice cream
buy	bill
look at	hot-dog
eat	flowers
~~drink~~	mobile

When the aliens arrived ...

1 Megan *was drinking some lemonade.*
2 Tom ……………
3 Mira ……………
4 William ……………
5 Scott ……………
6 Owen ……………
7 Jenny ……………
8 Paula ……………

Grammar Past continuous

■ **2 Make the questions and answer them about yourself.**

1 eat breakfast / 7 a.m. this morning
Were you eating breakfast at 7 a.m. this morning? — Yes I was. / No, I wasn't. I was sleeping.
2 study maths / 11 a.m. yesterday
3 watch TV / 11 p.m. yesterday
4 speak on the telephone / 6 p.m. yesterday
5 sleep / 6 a.m. this morning
6 do homework / 9 p.m. yesterday

END OF REVISION SECTION

■ **3** **Below are some sentences from the diary of one of the men on Lewis and Clarke's great adventure. Read *Westward ho! – from St. Louis to The Pacific Coast* in your Student's Book again and choose the right dates from the box.**

~~August 1805~~
October 1804
March 1806
May 1804
August 1806
November 1805
October 1805
June 1805
September 23rd 1806

August 1805 ....
'Luckily the Indians are friendly. Tomorrow one of them has promised to show us a way through the mountains.'

....
'We met our Indian friends again. It's good to see their faces again. We know we are nearly home now.'

....
'Today we must start the journey back. The journey will be long and dangerous. I miss my wife and children and can't wait to see them.'

....
'Today we finally saw what we have been looking for – the ocean. At last we have crossed this huge country of ours and it is beautiful.'

....
'Home at last. Today is the happiest day of my life. But part of me is sad because I know I can never have an adventure like this again.'

....
'After nearly three months we have finally arrived. We are hungry but happy to be here. It was a difficult journey.'

....
'The waterfalls are incredible. I've never seen anything so wonderful. The only problem is: how will we get the boats around them?'

....
'Winter is coming and we must build a shelter* before the snow arrives. The local Indians, who have been very friendly are helping us with the job.'

....
'Today we finally set off westwards on the Missouri River. Who knows where our great adventure will take us?'

● **4** **Here are some drawings from the diary. Write a date under each one.**

VOCABULARY
***shelter** – Unterschlupf

....

....

....

▶ SB p. 22

■ **5** **Read Shireen's letter and complete it with the words in the box.**

slept
suffered
hired
went
met
took
get
got

Dear Ahmed,
We're having a really great time here in Peru. It's such an amazing place and it's so good to ¹.................................. away from London for a while. The local people are really friendly and we've ².................................. some lovely people here. We spent the first week in Lima and then we ³.................................. a car to see a bit more of the country. We've spent some nights in hotels but we've also ⁴.................................. in tents too.*
Yesterday we ⁵.................................. up to Machu Picchu – it's fantastic. It's an ancient city high up in the Andes. Unfortunately mum ⁶.................................. from a bit of altitude sickness, so we couldn't stay too long. Guess what we saw on the way down? A snake. I ⁷.................................. really close to it. I ⁸.................................. some really good photos. I'll show you them when we get back. Can't wait to see you.
Love Shireen

VOCABULARY: *tent – Zelt

● **6** **Read 'My best trip ever' and 'Camping in Scotland' in your Student's Book (p. 24/25) again. Who took each of these photos? Write *the boy* or *the girl* under each one.**

....

....

....

....

....

● **7** **Read 'My best trip ever' and 'Camping in Scotland' again. Tick T (*True*) or F (*False*).**

		T	F
1	When the girl arrived at the farm she didn't know anyone.	☐	☐
2	She made friends with a girl called Wendy.	☐	☐
3	She rode her horse on grass and sand.	☐	☐
4	She had great weather all holiday.	☐	☐
5	The boy already knew how to climb when he went to Glencoe.	☐	☐
6	He wasn't very good at cooking for himself.	☐	☐
7	Fergus and Douglas helped him put up his tent.	☐	☐
8	The boy found the climb back down Agag's Groove harder than the climb up it.	☐	☐

► SB p. 23

★ **8** **Read the story and choose the correct options to complete the sentences.**

Going to Granada

A few years ago our daughter Lucille went to Managua, the capital of Nicaragua, to work on a project. A chocolate company from Birmingham wanted to buy cocoa from Nicaraguan farmers and she had to go to farms and talk to the managers there. She really wanted us to visit her.

"We don't speak any Spanish, and we don't like hot countries very much," I said to my husband. "Let's go anyway," my husband said. "It would make her happy." So we went.

It was a long flight and to Managua. Then Lucille said "Let's take a bus to Granada."

We went to the bus station, but it didn't look like a bus station at all. There in the middle of a square were two old VW-buses. Before we could say anything, two men pushed us into the first bus. We gave them some money, bought a bottle of water from a kid – and off we went. The road was bad and sometimes small animals ran onto it. The driver didn't care. He just went as fast as the bus would let him. Even my husband, who likes to think of himself as a Formula 1 driver, closed his eyes at times, because he didn't want to see how fast we were going. Only Lucille and the other passengers were having a good time.

When we got off the bus in Granada, all we heard were shouts of "Taxi, taxi," but Lucille said: "Let's take the bus to the centre." The bus was a small open van* with a wooden bench* at each side. We got in. Then some more people got in and then some more. After 10 minutes it left. But it soon stopped to let more people get in. In the end, nobody could move any longer. "I know we have to get off at the next stop," Lucille said, "but I don't know how." "I'll just sit here," my husband said "and get off when everybody else does." "No way," I said. "I want to go to the hotel right now." I got up – and the people all moved aside a little. I don't know how, but in the end we got off the van with all our bags – and we were in front of the hotel. The hotel was lovely – large rooms, a swimming pool and lots of beautiful trees and flowers. But getting there was quite a journey, believe me.

VOCABULARY
***van** – Lieferwagen
***bench** – Sitzbank

1 The story is written by
- a) ☐ Lucille.
- b) ☐ her mother.
- c) ☐ her father.

2 Her parents went to visit her because
- a) ☐ they wanted to practise their Spanish.
- b) ☐ they really needed a holiday anyway.
- c) ☐ they wanted to make her happy.

3 At the bus station they say that
- a) ☐ there weren't any buses there.
- b) ☐ it was very different to bus stations in the UK.
- c) ☐ there were lots of people there.

4 For the mother the journey to Granada was
- a) ☐ fast and dangerous.
- b) ☐ slow and dirty.
- c) ☐ fun and exciting.

5 The van they took was
- a) ☐ slow.
- b) ☐ full of people.
- c) ☐ cheap.

6 Lucille's father wanted to get off the bus
- a) ☐ at the hotel.
- b) ☐ when it was empty.
- c) ☐ and get a taxi.

▶ SB pp. **24, 25**

★ **9** **Write a report about an interesting journey you have taken. Say:**

- where you went
- what were the best/worst things about your journey
- how long you were away
- if you would go there again etc.

■ **10** **John wants to by a ticket from the man at the ticket office. Put the dialogue in order.**

☐ **Man** Let me see. That's £86.
☐ **Man** OK, there's a train at 3.15. And when do you want to come back?
☐ **Man** OK. So that's a return leaving today and coming back Sunday.
1 **Man** Hello, can I help you?
☐ **Man** Sure. When do you want to leave?
☐ **John** What! I think I'm going to take the bus.
☐ **John** On Sunday.
☐ **John** Today about 3 p.m.
☐ **John** That's right. How much is it?
☐ **John** Yes, I'd like to buy a return ticket to Bristol.

★ **11** **"The Longest Journey" – Write a short story.**

GRAMMAR while, before, after

■ **12** **Look at the pictures and complete the sentences with *while*, *after* or *before*.**

1 .... we were having breakfast, we were watching TV.

2 .... we had breakfast we watched some TV.

3 .... we had breakfast we watched some TV.

4 I lost my keys .... I was getting off the bus.

5 I lost my keys .... I got off the bus.

6 I lost my keys .... I got off the bus.

▶ SB pp. 23, 27

13 **Choose the correct option to complete the sentences.**

A terrible flight

1 *While / During* I was shutting my suitcase, it broke.
2 *While / During* the trip to the airport, the car broke down.
3 There was lots of turbulence* *while / during* the flight.
4 *While / During* I was reading my book, the lights went out.
5 I dropped my Coke *while / during* the meal and got my trousers all wet.
6 A baby kept crying *while / during* the film and I couldn't hear anything.
7 The man in front started snoring *while / during* I was trying to get to sleep.
8 *While / During* I was waiting at passport control, I discovered my passport was still on the plane.

VOCABULARY
***turbulence** – Turbulenz

14 **Write sentences. How long does it take you to …**

1 get to school?
It takes me … minutes. ....
2 do your homework each night?
....
3 fall asleep at night?
....
4 decide what to wear to go to a party?
....

Word File

Travelling

- **suffer from altitude sickness**
- **land**
- **fly** (back)
- **sleep in tents**
- it **takes** an hour
- **get on** (a plane)
- **set off** (for work)
- **get to** (the airport)
- **talk to** each other
- **get off** (the plane)
- **get into** (a car)
- **get out of** (the car)
- **get close to** (alligators)
- **meet** other **people**
- **be with** each other
- **take** a trip
- **hire** a car
- **drive** (home)
- **get away**
- **take off**

SB p. 27

MORE Words and Phrases

■ 1	accompany sb	*They had 45 men to accompany them.*	jdn begleiten
	across	*They travelled across the Rocky Mountains.*	über
	after	*Soon after they crossed the river there was the next big problem.*	nachdem
	by sea	*Travellling by sea takes longer than by plane.*	auf dem Seeweg, per Schiff
	countryside	*Lewis was studying the countryside.*	Land(schaft)
	expedition	*Lewis and Clark went on an expedition to the west.*	Expedition, Forschungsreise
	explore	*They explored the land.*	erforschen, erkunden
	explorer	*In 1804 the two explorers left St. Louis.*	Forscher/in
	sail	*They wanted to sail back by sea.*	segeln
	trail	*There was a trail across the Rockies.*	Weg, Pfad
	tribe	*They reached the Indian tribe of the Mandan.*	Stamm (Volk)
	unknown	*They found unknown plants on their journey.*	unbekannt, nicht bekannt
● 2	**for a while**	*We want to relax for a while.*	eine Weile
	prefer sth	*Which of the trips would you prefer?*	etwas vorziehen, bevorzugen
	scenery	*You can see the beautiful scenery from the mountain.*	Landschaft
● 4	**passenger**	*The plane had 200 passengers.*	Fahrgast; Passagier
	rest	*After a rest, she flew back.*	(Ruhe)pause
■ 5	**be afraid (of)**	*She was afraid because she was alone.*	Angst haben/sich fürchten (vor)
	cliff	*When you climb a cliff, don´t look down!*	Klippe, Kliff
	experienced	*The guides were experienced climbers.*	erfahren, geschult
	fortunately	*Fortunately we had good weather.*	zum Glück
	gear	*To go rock climbing you need the right gear.*	Ausrüstung, Sachen
	gradually	*Gradually we became better climbers.*	allmählich
	make friends	*And I soon made friends with the people on the farm.*	sich anfreunden
	put up	*We put up the fence.*	aufhängen; hier: aufstellen
	rock face	*We had to walk up the rock face first.*	Bergwand
	victory	*We celebrated our victory at the top.*	Sieg
	view	*The view of the mountains is stunning.*	Sicht; (Aus)blick, Aussicht
● 7	bank holiday	*Nobody goes to work in the UK on a bank holiday.*	öffentlicher Feiertag
	cheap	*Dad's booked one of those cheap flights.*	billig, preiswert
	customer	*Our customers are very happy with our new machine.*	Kunde/Kundin
	departure	*Check-in is two hours before departure.*	Abreise
	train	*The train left the station at 5 p. m.*	Zug
● 8	**delayed**	*Our flight was delayed by an hour.*	verspätet, verzögert
	passport	*I forgot my passport and couldn't fly.*	Reisepass
	smell	*The food on the plane didn't smell good.*	Geruch
	traveller	*Many travellers come here by train.*	Reisende/r
● 9	**experience**	*Would you talk about a bad experience?*	Erfahrung
	impossible	*Who will win? It's impossible to say.*	unmöglich

UNIT 4 Dangerous animals

Revision Vocabulary

1 Complete the dialogue with the phrases in the box.

go up to the mountains
meet new people
hire a car
Get close
suffer from altitude sickness
get away
Sleep in a tent
take lots of photos

Brenda What's the matter Jake? You don't look so happy.
Jake It's school, Aunt Brenda. I've got loads of tests coming up.
Brenda But then you're on holiday, right?
Jake Yeah.
Brenda You need to [1]... from here. Why don't you [2]... , jump in it and see where it takes you.
Jake Hire a car? I haven't got enough money for that.
Brenda OK, so take a train and [3]... for some fresh air. [4]... to nature.
Jake I can't. I [5]... .
Brenda OK, so go down to the beach and stay in a hotel.
Jake I haven't got enough money to stay in a hotel.
Brenda OK, so go camping. [6]... . It's a great way to [7]... .
Jake That's not a bad idea. I just might do that.
Brenda And don't forget to [8]... to show me when you get back.

Grammar after, before, during, while

2 Complete the sentences with *after, before, during* or *while*.

Killer Rabbits was on at the cinema. I had to see it. [1]...................... I went to the cinema, I phoned Sue and asked her to come with me. She told me three times that she doesn't like horror films [2]...................... the phone call. [3]...................... she finished talking I promised to see another film with her. We met at the cinema. [4]...................... we were waiting to buy our tickets I saw Jim. He likes horror films.

I said goodbye to Sue and then Jim and I went to see *Killer Rabbits*. Sue never spoke to me again [5]...................... that. Did I do something wrong?

[6]...................... the film started I bought a giant bag of popcorn. Unfortunately I dropped most of it [7]...................... I was watching the film. The film was great. I only closed my eyes fifty times [8]...................... it and I didn't sleep for two weeks [9]...................... it. Now that's what I call a good horror film.

END OF REVISION SECTION

● **3 Put the dialogues in the correct order.**

1
- [ ] **A** Just alright?
- [ ] **B** Yes, I saw it on DVD a few days ago.
- [1] **A** Have you seen *Madagascar*?
- [ ] **B** Well, I like action films better.
- [ ] **A** Did you like it?
- [ ] **B** Yes, it's alright.

2
- [ ] **B** No, but I'd like to see it.
- [ ] **B** You mean *Finding Nemo*.
- [ ] **A** Well let's get it out on DVD then.
- [ ] **A** Yes, that's right.
- [1] **A** Have you seen that film about the fish that's looking for his son?

3
- [ ] **A** Well you must. It's awesome.
- [ ] **B** A Shark's what?
- [ ] **B** No, I don't think I have.
- [1] **A** Have you seen *A Shark's Tale*?
- [ ] **A** *A Shark's Tale*. It's a really funny animated film.

■ **4 Find 12 adjectives in the word snake.**

fantasticamazinginterestingawesomegreathorribleboringscarycutefunnygrossexciting

5 Choose five of the adjectives from the word snake and use them to describe films you have seen in the last few months.

'Charlie and the Chocolate Factory' was awesome. *'Finding Nemo' was cute.*

....

....

....

....

....

■ **6 Read the story about Bethany Hamilton in your Student's Book (p. 30/31) again. Are these sentences true or false?**

		T	F
1	The accident happened on October 29th.	☐	☐
2	Bethany's mother didn't really want to stay at the beach.	☐	☐
3	Bethany's family weren't really happy about her dreams of being a surfer.	☐	☐
4	There were a lot of big waves that day.	☐	☐
5	Bethany kept calm after the shark bit her.	☐	☐
6	The ambulance arrived really quickly.	☐	☐
7	The doctor told her never to surf again.	☐	☐
8	People helped her and her family a lot after the accident.	☐	☐

▶ SB pp. 29, 30

★ **7** **Read the text. Where in the text do the missing sentences below belong? Write numbers.**

dangerous creatures

Are you looking for dangerous animals? Then Australia is the country for you. Many of the most dangerous animals in the world live there. [ ] The travel writer Bill Bryson once said that some of the animals in Australia are so deadly that when they bite you, you won't have time to finish your sentence. Before you can say "Look there's a deadly sn …," you're dead!

Some of Australia's dangerous creatures need no introduction. The Saltwater crocodile [ ] is one of the most famous. Usually they are around 4m long but sometimes they reach a huge 7m. They are found on the north-eastern coast of Australia but also for up to a 100 kilometres or more away from the sea. They are often hiding in rivers and lakes in the area. This is why on most boat tours they tell you not to hold your arm above the water, because there might be a crocodile ready to jump out of the water [ ].

Other killers are snakes and spiders. The best-known deadly spider is the Red-back spider. It lives in city areas, so you're not safe even in your own home. Snakes usually leave people alone, they only attack when they feel they are in danger. The Brown snake and the Tiger snake are the most dangerous snakes [ ].

But the most dangerous animal in Australia is not the crocodile or the spider or the snake: it's the jellyfish. For example, the Box jellyfish*. It's about 80 cm long and lives in the Great Barrier Reef. Never let this creature sting* you. You can stop breathing* and die in less than three minutes. Some say the Irukandji jellyfish is even more dangerous because it's only 2,5 cm long and very difficult to see in the water.

[ ] Watch out also for the beautiful Blue-ring octopus. Its bite can kill. And then there's the stonefish – its poison can kill a man in two hours.

But don't start thinking about not going to Australia. [ ] Just take care and when you see a sign such as "Danger – crocodiles!", don't jump into the water!

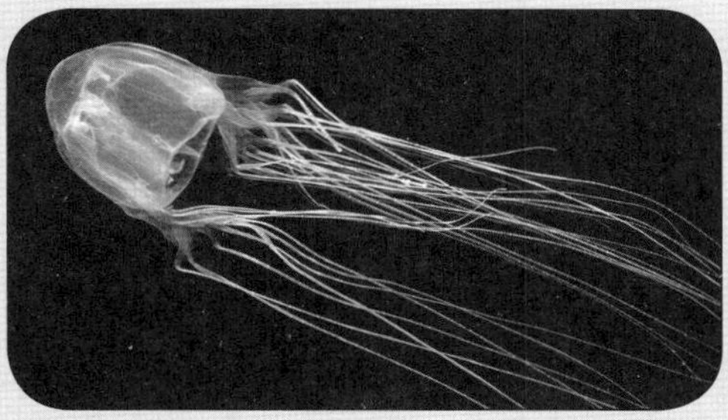

VOCABULARY
***jellyfish** – Qualle
***sting** – verbrennen
***breathe** – atmen

1 But jellyfish aren't the only dangers in the sea.
2 It's a beautiful country and creatures like these are what help make it so wonderful.
3 For example, six of the ten most deadliest snakes in the world come from Australia.
4 and bite off your arm
5 , but if you get to a doctor right away, you won't die from these snake bites
6 , the world's largest reptile,

▶ SB pp. **28, 32**

8 Writing. Read the following email and then answer it.

Hi Karl,

You know we're coming to Austria next month, and we're also doing mountain trips and stuff like that. Dad's a bit worried about the wild animals. He wants to know – is there anything dangerous? Snakes or spiders? (I'm soooo scared of spiders.) Is there anything we should bring? I read somewhere that there are bears in Austria. No crocodiles and tigers though, eh? Only in the zoo, I read.

Anyway, please let me know.

Love,

Tiffany

9 Rewrite the sentences so that they mean the same.

Example: Anna is older than Janet. → *Janet is not as old as Anna.*

1 Squash is more exciting than tennis.

....

....

2 Rome is bigger than Naples.

....

3 Greece is hotter than Finland.

....

4 Spanish is easier than Hungarian.

....

5 Natasha is friendlier than Victoria.

....

6 The hotel in Edinburgh was worse than the hotel in Glasgow.

....

....

7 Fantasy films are more exciting than romantic films.

....

....

8 Cartoons are funnier than detective films.

....

....

Grammar Comparatives and superlatives

10 Complete the sentences with a superlative.

1 **A** Charles and George are good at maths.
  B Yeah but I'm ......*the best*....... .

2 **A** Tammy and Georgina have got really cute dogs.
  B Yeah, but my dog is ....

3 **A** Nigel and Geoff girlfriend's are really pretty.
  B Yeah, but my girlfriend is ....

4 **A** Paul and Steve have got really cool bikes.
  B Yeah, but my bike is ....

5 **A** The teacher said that the twins are really intelligent.
  B Yeah, but I'm ....

6 **A** My mum and dad have got really expensive cars.
  B Yeah, but my dad's car is ....

▶ SB pp. 32, 35

■ **11 Complete the text using the correct form of the adjectives in brackets.**

Sequels* are never usually as [1] .... (good) as the first film in a series. For example, *Speed* was an [2] .... (awesome) film. *Speed II* was [3] .... (bad) film ever made. *Spiderman* is [4] .... (exciting) superhero film I've seen. *Spiderman II* is [5] .... (boring).
Of course, this isn't always true. What about *Shrek*, for example. I think that *Shrek II* is [6] .... (good) than *Shrek*. I think that it is [7] .... (funny) and I also think the story is [8] .... (interesting). Don't get me wrong. I like *Shrek*, it's a [9] .... (great) film. It's a lot [10] .... (intelligent) than most Hollywood films. But I just don't think it is as [11] .... (funny) as the second part. I think *Shrek II* is [12] .... (great) animated film ever made.

VOCABULARY
***sequel** – Folge, Fortsetzung

★ **12 Look at the information in the table. Are the sentences true or false?**

A

speed	Year	length	comfort	price
160km/h	2004	3m	★★★	£8,000

B

speed	Year	length	comfort	price
180km/h	1985	4m	★★	£8,000

C

speed	Year	length	comfort	price
200km/h	1967	3m	★	£25,000

		T	F
1	Car C is more expensive than car B but not as expensive as car A.	☐	☐
2	Car A is faster than car B but not as fast as car C.	☐	☐
3	Car B is older than car A but not as old as car C.	☐	☐
4	Car A is as long as car B but not as long as car C.	☐	☐
5	Car C is more comfortable than car A and B.	☐	☐
6	Car A is as expensive as car B.	☐	☐
7	Car B is the longest.	☐	☐
8	Car C is the fastest.	☐	☐
9	Car C is as new as car B, but Car A is the newest.	☐	☐
10	Car A is the most uncomfortable.	☐	☐

★ **13 Correct the false sentences above. Write them down.**

▶ SB p. **35**

■ 14 **What do you think of these paintings? Write sentences to compare them. Use the adjectives in the box to help you.**

Painting A is the oldest. ....

I think painting B is the most beautiful. ....

old
beautiful
good
modern
exciting
interesting
ugly

....

....

....

....

....

....

....

....

Everyday English Dangerous dogs

Look at the phrases on p. 34 in your Student's Book again. Use them to complete the dialogues.

1 **A** Did you hear Jenny playing the guitar? I think she's hopeless.

B I don't agree. .... – she's not a good player, but she's not hopeless!

2 **A** Do you think we should get a dog for grandma?

B Well, ... It'd be great for her to have a pet for company, but maybe a dog would be too much work for her.

3 **A** Do you think Mrs Morrison would look after Blackie while we're away?

B .... She said No last time we asked her.

A Yeah, ... Maybe we need to ask else.

▶ SB pp. 34, 35

MORE Words and Phrases

●	1	bee	*A swarm of bees has arrived.*	Biene
		cockroach	*Cockroaches live in cities and are hard to kill.*	Küchenschabe, Kakerlake
		deadly	*The bite of the taipan snake is deadly.*	tödlich
		rabies	*Rabies is a very dangerous illness in animals.*	Tollwut
■	2	**own**	*Do you own a pet? Is it a dog or a cat?*	besitzen
●	5	**badly**	*She was bleeding badly.*	sehr; hier: stark
		bleed	*You can get killed by bleeding to death.*	bluten
		bleeding	*He helped control the bleeding.*	Blutung
		calm	*In a loud but calm voice she said what happened.*	ruhig, gelassen
		contact sb	*An organization contacted her.*	sich mit jdm in Verbindung setzen
		fear	*Her dreams are bigger than her fear.*	Angst; fürchten
		nightmare	*A dream can turn into a nightmare.*	Albtraum
		offer	*They offered her a job as a photographer.*	anbieten
●	6	**attack**	*She became the victim of a shark attack.*	Angriff
■	7	**advise sb against sth**	*Gillian advises against swimming with sharks.*	jdm von etwas abraten, jdn vor etwas warnen
		bull shark	*Is the most feared shark the bull shark?*	Bullenhai
		defend	*Sharks kill to defend their territory.*	verteidigen
		mistake sth for sth	*Sharks mistake humans for seals.*	etwas mit etwas verwechseln
		seal	*Seals and sea lions are the great white shark's food.*	Seehund, Robbe
		tiger shark	*The tiger shark has its name because it looks like a tiger.*	Tigerhai
●	8	croc (crocodile)	*Crocs have a big and dangerous mouth.*	Krokodil
	D3	Don't **get** me **wrong.**	*Now – don't get me wrong, it's terrible. But not that bad.*	Versteh mich nicht falsch!
		Good point.	*We need his opinion. – Good point.*	'Ganz richtig! Stimmt!'

UNIT 5 London calling!

Revision Vocabulary

■ 1 **Cross out the adjective that is wrong in each sentence.**

1 It was really *funny / boring / great*. We laughed a lot.
2 And then the lights went out. It was so *nice / scary / horrible* I wanted to scream but I couldn't.
3 There was this dog with ten lovely babies. They were so *horrible / nice / scary*.
4 It was so *uninteresting / boring / fantastic* that I nearly fell asleep.
5 I thought the TV report on crocodiles was really *interesting / great / boring*. I want to find out more about them.

Grammar Comparatives and superlatives

■ 2 **Complete the text with the correct form of the adjectives in brackets.**

Last year I went on a big tour of Europe with my family. It was [1].. (awesome). We visited lots of great cities, but I think [2].. (good) was probably London. I know it's not as [3].. (beautiful) Paris and it's not as [4].. (ancient) as Rome, but there was something so special about it. I think it's the people. They're [5].. (friendly) than the Parisians and the Romans. They're always doing something. But it's not just Londoners, you find people from all over the world there. It's such an [6].. (exciting) city. I don't think the other cities are as [7].. (exciting) as London. It's difficult to get [8].. (bored) in London. A famous writer called Samuel Johnson once said that when you get [9].. (tired) of London, then you are tired of life, too. I think he's right.

■ 3 **Rewrite each sentence so that it means the same as the original. Use the word in brackets.**

1 He's not as intelligent as his brother. (more)
His brother's more intelligent than him.
2 The blue watch is more expensive than the red one. (not as)
3 The first film in the series was better than the other two. (best)
4 I think tennis and football are both boring. (as)
5 There last CD was better than this one. (good)
6 I don't think there's a taller building in the world than this one. (tallest)

END OF REVISION SECTION

4 **Read the text *Beside the River Thames* in your Student's Book (p. 38/39) again. Which of the places did each of these tourists visit?**

We had to wait a long time to get in, but it was great to see all the royal* history.

We were really lucky because there was a boat coming just as we arrived there.

There's some amazing underwater life to see there. It's difficult to believe it was where the mayor* of London once had his offices.

This place is modern British architecture* at its best!

We didn't see any famous politicians, but it was fantastic just to be in the place where British politics is decided.

The ride's actually quite slow, so you have lots of time to see everything.

While I watched the play, I almost believed I was back in 16th century England.

I still can't believe that I paid nothing to see all these wonderful paintings.

VOCABULARY
***royal** – königlich
***mayor** – Bürgermeister
***architecture** – Architektur

5 **Use the clues to complete the crossword and find the secret word.**
(Clue: It's the name of one of London's railway stations.)

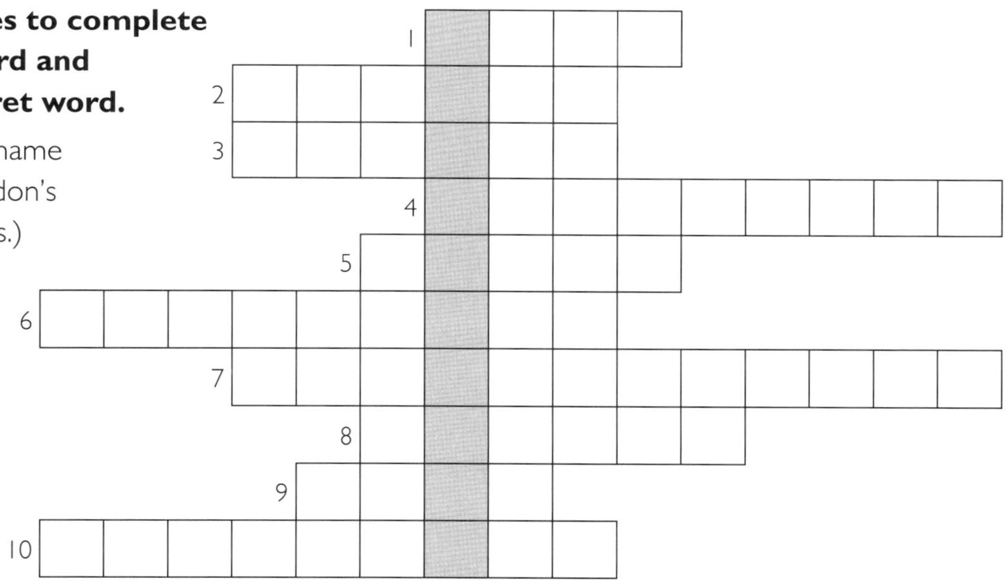

1 Relax and watch the world go by in Hyde ...
2 Take a photo of Nelson and his lions in Trafalgar ...
3 Watch boats sail under Tower ...
4 Hang out in Soho, one of London's most famous ...
5 Take a boat trip on the ... Thames.
6 Take a train ride from one of London's many ...
7 Visit the Tate. One of the best ... in the world.
8 Walk down Oxford ... and look in the shops.
9 Buy something at Harrods, the world's most famous ...
10 Take a look at some of London's modern ... like The Gherkin and Canary Wharf.

SB p. 39

★ **6** **Read the dialogue and complete it with the words in the box.**

younger which the who isn't more bought tell are why during after

Julian What [1]................................ you reading?

Sandra It's a book of stories about London. I'm reading the story of Dick Whittington.

Julian The poor boy [2]................................ became mayor of London?

Sandra That's right. Except he was never poor. Did you know he became mayor of London four times [3]................................ his life?

Julian Really? I just remember the story my mum told me when I was [4]................................ . There was something about a cat.

Sandra That's right. The story says that he [5] .... a cat for a penny and sold it for lots and lots of money.

Julian Is it true?

Sandra No. He had a cat, but it didn't make him rich. A lot of that children's story [6]................................ true.

Julian Like what?

Sandra Like that famous bit about the bells [7]................................ told him to go back to London and find his fortune*.

Julian That never happened?

Sandra No.

Julian Okay, so [8]................................ me the real story then.

Sandra Well, as you know, "Dick" is the short form of Richard. Richard Whittington lived around 1400 and he was a very rich man. He was one of [9]................................ richest men in London. It was King Richard II who made him Lord Mayor first. He did a lot of business with the royal family. Later he did business with King Henry IV and the people made him their mayor three [10]................................ times.

Julian So it was all about money. That's not very romantic, is it?

Sandra No, but it's interesting. [11]................................ Dick died in 1423 he left a lot of money that went to poor people.

Julian That explains [12]................................ he was so popular.

Sandra And it also explains why he's so famous.

VOCABULARY
***fortune** – Glück

■ **7** **Read the dialogue again. Tick the following sentences T (*True*) or F (*False*).**

		T	F
1	Dick Whittington's family wasn't very rich.	☐	☐
2	He was mayor of London four times.	☐	☐
3	He had a cat.	☐	☐
4	His cat made him a lot of money.	☐	☐
5	Bells told him to go and live in London.	☐	☐
6	He knew kings.	☐	☐
7	He gave a lot of money away.	☐	☐
8	He was a real person.	☐	☐

▶ SB pp. 39, 40

8 **Read Susan's letter and put these photos in the order in which she took them.**

Dear Aunt Helen,

I've just got back from a school trip to London. We were there for three days and I can tell you – it was really tiring (but it was pretty cool, too). We were with our teachers most of the time, so we didn't have much free time, but we saw all the famous places. That made my mum happy. Actually, some of them were quite interesting. I liked St. Paul's Cathedral best. We went there on the second morning we were there. We walked up all the 500+ steps, and when we got to the top, there was a great view of London. It was a really sunny day, so we could see far more than the morning before, when we were on the London Eye. After St Paul's we went to see a film in that big cinema in Leicester Square – but the tickets were very expensive.

On our first evening we went to the Globe Theatre and saw a Shakespeare play. It was called 'A Comedy of Errors.' Okay, the language was kind of strange, but the actors* were really great. And the actors who played the twins really looked the same. They were great. We laughed quite a lot. The only thing I hated was that we had to stand for two hours. But you could walk around a bit, so it was okay in the end.

The best thing of all was shopping, of course! The teachers gave us a couple of hours of free time every day, and we went to Covent Garden (I bought a shirt there), and to Camden Market. I bought a T-shirt and Lucy bought a funny hat. It's really colourful and has got a plastic flower sticking out from it!

Yesterday was our last day and we went to the Science Museum. Now, that really is a great museum. After that we had an hour to wait, so I bought this card and thought I'd write to you. Unfortunately, I got talking with Lucy and had to write it at home.

Love, Susan

VOCABULARY
***actor / actress** – Schauspieler/Schauspielerin

9 **Read the text again. Are the sentences true or false?**

		T	F
1	Susan found the trip very tiring.	☐	☐
2	Susan really enjoyed all the sights.	☐	☐
3	They didn't have great weather the day they went on the London Eye.	☐	☐
4	Susan thought the cinema was very expensive.	☐	☐
5	They didn't have seats at the theatre.	☐	☐
6	The actresses in the play were twins.	☐	☐
7	Susan only bought clothes in London.	☐	☐
8	She wrote the card outside the Science Museum.	☐	☐

▶ SB pp. **40, 41, 42, 43**

■ **10 Look at the pictures. Write a story.**

Grammar Relative pronouns

● **11 Write *which* or *who* in the spaces to complete the questions.**

1 What's the name of the river .... flows through London?
a) ☐ the Severn
b) ☐ the Dee
c) ☐ the Thames

2 Many tourists .... go to London want to see Big Ben. But what is Big Ben?
a) ☐ a clock
b) ☐ a tower
c) ☐ a bell

3 What is the name of the giant wheel .... you can find on the South Bank of the river?
a) ☐ the London Eye
b) ☐ the London Wheel
c) ☐ the London Roundabout

4 What's the name of the architect .... designed City Hall?
a) ☐ Charles Dickens
b) ☐ Norman Foster
c) ☐ Tim Vickery

5 What do you call the guards .... protect the Crown Jewels?
a) ☐ Steakmen
b) ☐ Porklovers
c) ☐ Beefeaters

6 Who was the famous writer .... kept a diary of London life in the 1600s?
a) ☐ Samuel Pepys
b) ☐ Christopher Wren
c) ☐ William Shakespeare

7 What's the name of the area of London .... was a flower market until about 40 years ago?
a) ☐ Covent Garden
b) ☐ Waterloo
c) ☐ Hyde Park

● **12 Now do the quiz. Tick the correct answers. All the answers are in your Student's Book.**

▶ SB pp. 40, 41, 42, 43, 45

● **13** **Put the words in order to make sentences.**

1 man / made the film / *Jurassic Park* / the / who / is / Spielberg

Spielberg is the man who made the film 'Jurassic Park.'

2 the girl / know / lives upstairs? / Do / that / you

....

3 to / this / goes / which / Piccadilly Circus? / Is / the bus

....

4 I've got / London. / lives / who / a / in / friend

....

5 you / you / much? / liked / T-shirt / which / Did / the / so / buy

....

6 the / Where's / this door? / who / key / the / has / to / woman

....

■ **14** **Write sentences like in the example in your exercise book. Use your own ideas.**

Example: *William Shakespeare is the man who wrote 'Romeo and Juliet'.*

Everyday English The raffle ticket

Look at the phrases on p. 44 in your Student's Book again.
Use them to complete the dialogues.

1 **A** If you want to buy yourself a new bike, why don't you earn some money by washing people's cars?

B .... But I'm not sure there are many people who want their car washed.

A Maybe not. But .... , isn't it?

2 **A** Mum? Can I go to Greece on a camping tour with my friends during the holidays?

B .... , Nick! You're only fourteen! Of course you can't go!

3 **A** Look, Ruby, help me tidy up the house and I'll take you to your favourite restaurant on Sunday.

B OK, Dad, but only if I can have a double portion of lemon ice cream!

A .... !

▶ SB p. 44

MORE Words and Phrases

●	1	in advance	*Book your ride in advance.*	im Voraus
		be (not) allowed to do sth	*I wasn't allowed to ride the London Eye.*	etwas (nicht) tun dürfen
		beside	*Some interesting buildings are right beside the River Thames.*	neben
		City Hall	*City Hall is where the town government meets.*	Stadtverwaltung; Rathaus
		collection	*The Tate Modern has a great collection of art.*	Sammlung
		entry	*Entry to the art gallery is free.*	Eintritt
		factory	*A place where different things are made.*	Fabrik; Werk
		gallery	*The old factory building is now an art gallery.*	Galerie
		get ready (for sth)	*Get ready for a long queue in front of the London Eye.*	sich (für etwas) bereitmachen
		giant wheel	*The London Eye is a giant wheel.*	Riesenrad
		government	*The British government meets in the Houses of Parliament.*	Regierung
		grow up	*London grew up around a river.*	erwachsen werden; hier: entstehen
		hand	*Big Ben's hands are 2.7 and 4.3 metres long.*	Zeiger (Uhr)
		the Houses of Parliament	*The most famous place in London.*	das Parlament (von Großbritannien)
		queue	*There's always a long queue at the Tower of London.*	Schlange, Reihe
		raise	*They raise the bridge to let ships go through.*	(an)heben, hochziehen
		stairs (pl)	*There are a lot of stairs to the top of the City Hall.*	Treppe
		theatre	*Shakespeare played in the Globe Theatre.*	Theater
		visitor	*Visitors can go in City Hall.*	Besucher/in
★	3b	district	*There are many great districts in London.*	Gebiet; Bezirk
		recommend	*I can recommend going to the park.*	empfehlen
	5	thrilling	*A ride on the London Eye can be thrilling.*	aufregend
	6	burn down	*Almost all the houses burned down.*	abbrennen
		century	*In the 17th century, London was a much smaller city.*	Jahrhundert
		narrow	*London had narrow streets and wooden houses.*	eng, schmal
		other	*The fire destroyed St. Paul's Cathedral and a lot of other buildings.*	weitere(r,s)
		rebuild	*Many people had to rebuild their houses.*	wieder aufbauen
		weak	*The fire was weak but became stronger.*	schwach
■	7	**be about**	*This museum is all about torture.*	handeln von
		entertainment	*Go to Covent Garden and watch the street entertainment.*	Unterhaltung
		market	*Covent Garden was a flower market.*	Markt
		memorial	*The memorial to Princess Diana is in Hyde Park.*	Denkmal
		torture (no pl)	*The London Dungeon was a prison famous for torture and death.*	Folter
		traffic	*There's a lot of traffic in London.*	Verkehr
■	DI	raffle	*I lost at the raffle.*	Tombola, Verlosung
		raffle ticket	*Let me see your raffle ticket. You won!*	Los

UNIT 6 What will happen if ...?

Revision Vocabulary

■ **1 Find eight things you can see in a city. Look in all directions!**

A	B	M	Q	S	P	D	F	O	L
X	R	P	T	E	E	R	T	S	M
C	I	T	O	W	E	R	G	Q	B
B	D	C	G	V	R	S	T	U	K
M	G	I	I	A	P	K	R	A	P
U	E	R	L	O	L	G	P	R	T
E	H	T	H	L	R	L	S	E	A
S	C	S	G	H	Q	Z	E	V	Y
U	Y	I	S	D	H	E	U	R	K
M	O	D	B	T	J	T	L	W	Y

★ **2 Test your geography. Use the words from the crossword to complete the sentences.**

1 The Prado .... is in Madrid.
2 The Golden Gate .... is in San Francisco.
3 Brooklyn is a .... of New York.
4 The Egypt .... is in Cairo.
5 Hyde .... is in London.
6 Tiananmen .... is in Beijing.
7 The Leaning .... is in Pisa.
8 The Champs Élysées is a .... in Paris.

Grammar Relative clauses

■ **3 Join the sentences together using *who* or *which*.**

1 A film director is a person. He / She makes films for the cinema.
A film director is a person who makes films for the cinema.
2 A dictionary is a book. It tells you what words mean.
3 A pilot is a person. He / She flies planes.
4 This is a shop. It sells computers.
5 Ferraris are Italian cars. They are very fast and powerful.
6 Londoners are people. They live in London.

END OF REVISION SECTION

4 Read 'The Monkey's Paw' again and choose the correct answer to the questions.

1 What does Neil think about the paw?

a) ☐ It's interesting.
b) ☐ It's gross.
c) ☐ It's wonderful.

2 Why didn't John Williams use the paw to make wishes?

a) ☐ He didn't believe it worked.
b) ☐ The old man told him not to.
c) ☐ He was scared something bad might happen.

3 Why isn't Neil scared to use the paw?

a) ☐ Because he doesn't think it'll work.
b) ☐ Because it might make him rich.
c) ☐ Because he used it a week ago and nothing happened.

4 How did Mr Morris' wish come true?

a) ☐ He won the lottery.
b) ☐ His son won the lottery.
c) ☐ He found the money.

5 What does Mrs Morris wish for?

a) ☐ To bring her son back to life.
b) ☐ To win some more money.
c) ☐ To destroy the paw.

5 Write a short text. You have found the monkey's paw. What are your three wishes? Write a story.

6 Complete the mini-dialogues with the lines from the box.

Because it'll bring me bad luck, of course.	I just don't. I think we make our own luck.
No, not at all.	Yes, I am. Very.
No, I don't. I think they're silly.	Well, for example, I never walk under a ladder.

A Are you superstitious?
B ....
A What sort of things do you do?
B ....
A Why not?
B ....

A Do you believe in superstitions?
B ....
A Why not?
B ....
A So you don't have a lucky charm*, for example?
B ....

VOCABULARY
***lucky charm** – Talisman

▶ SB p. 48

■ **7** **Read the story and complete it with the words in the box.**

bad
wished
brings
good
come
made
make
for
sad

It was the day before the most important test of the year. Maths! I hate maths. I just don't understand it. All those numbers. Give me words. I love words.

I was looking at my book on the desk and trying to study. But I just didn't understand it. I kept thinking about my birthday on Friday. Get a bad mark in my maths test and no party. I was [1]...................... . Then I remembered. Don't you get one wish for every birthday? I know, I'll [2]...................... my wish now, three days before!

I looked at my book and I [3]...................... a wish. I wished [4]...................... the best birthday party ever and then I made a second wish. Please, please let me get the best mark in the class. Better than Kate Holmes, better than James Love, better than all those clever kids who always get the top marks. Then I went to bed. I was tired from all the wishing.

The next day I woke up and went to school. I was nervous. It was test day and I didn't know anything. I put the picture of my dog on the desk. It's my lucky charm and it always [5]...................... me [6]...................... luck. It was very difficult.

The next day I got to school and I was really nervous. Results. Was this the end of my party? We got to the classroom, but Miss Chappell was not there. The headmaster arrived. Miss Chappell was ill. Results only on Monday. I was happy!

The party was great. Everyone was there. Kate Holmes and James Love talked about the maths test all the time. I didn't care. I just danced.

So did the wishes [7]...................... true? I had the best party ever, that's true. And the second wish? Well on Monday morning Miss Chappell was there. I got my results. 33.33% exactly. The worst result in the class. Yes, it was that [8]...................... !

■ **8** **Read the story again and put the following sentences in the correct order.**

☐ She had a great time at the party.
☐ She did her test.
☐ She didn't pass the maths test.
☐ She went to bed.
☐ She made a birthday wish.
☐ She got her results.
[1] Jenny was trying to study.
☐ Her teacher was ill.

★ **9** **Write a short story called 'A wish come true'. Use the picture to help you with the beginning.**

▶ SB p. 48

■ **10** **Read about superstitions from all over the world and write the name of the country under each picture.**

....

....

....

Some people believe: others don't!

Hironobu Akira

In Japan there are a lot of superstitions. I'd like to tell you about one of them.

There is a superstition about a white snake. What people say is this: if you find a white snake, you will be lucky in life. White snakes carry good luck. Some people even put up a picture of a white snake on a wall in their living room. Some people believe the snake is an animal of God, so they never kill snakes. I have never seen a white snake. There are not many of them.

Carmita Gonzales

In Mexico, some women think that a statue of San Antonio can help them to find a boyfriend. They go and buy the statue and then they put it in their bedroom and light a candle in front of it. Then they need to say a prayer* and ask San Antonio to make their wish come true. If they repeat this every day for two weeks, they will find a boyfriend.

I haven't got a boyfriend at the moment, but I don't believe that San Antonio can help me. I don't believe in superstitions.

Luis Andrade

There are lots of superstitions in Spain. Let me tell you about one. In the city where I live, in Salamanca, there is a famous university. There are many students there and they have a lot of superstitions. Near one of the doors of the university there is a frog on the wall. The frog is made of stone. When students have an important test, they come to this door. They touch the frog with their hands because they believe that this will bring good luck for the test. If they forget to do this, they won't get a good mark in the test.

VOCABULARY: *prayer – Gebet

● **11** **Decide if the sentences are true or false.**

		T	F
1	In Japan people are quite superstitious.	☐	☐
2	Some people in Japan keep pet snakes in their living room.	☐	☐
3	There are a lot of white snakes in Japan.	☐	☐
4	San Antonio only helps women.	☐	☐
5	You have to say a prayer to San Antonio for 10 nights if you want him to help you.	☐	☐
6	Carmita is going to buy a statue of San Antonio.	☐	☐
7	A lot of students live in Salamanca.	☐	☐
8	The frog on the door of the university is made of stone.	☐	☐
9	The frog helps students to pass their tests.	☐	☐

★ **12** **Find out about a superstition one of your family members has. Then write about it.**

▶ SB pp. 49, 50

Grammar 1st Conditional

● **13** **Match the sentence halves.**

1 If you wear that shirt,	☐ it'll bite you.
2 If you invite her to the cinema,	☐ will you be at home?
3 If you touch that dog,	☐ he'll have an accident.
4 If it's hot tomorrow,	☐ we'll be home by ten.
5 If I phone you at nine,	☐ you'll look really good.
6 If he drives that fast,	☐ will you buy some chocolate for me?
7 If we leave now,	☐ we'll go to the beach.
8 If I give you some money,	☐ I'm sure she'll say 'yes'.

● **14** **Underline the correct forms.**

1 **A** Come on. Hurry up.
B Don't worry. If we *miss* / *will miss* the bus, we *take* / *will take* a taxi.

2 **A** I don't want to eat an orange, mum.
B But if you *don't eat* / *won't eat* fruit, you *get* / *will get* a cold.

3 **A** I'm sorry. I'm really busy.
B Oh please. If you *help* / *will help* me, I *lend* / *will lend* you that Beyoncé CD.

4 **A** Jeff eats too many sweets.
B I know. If he *doesn't stop* / *won't stop* eating sweets, he *has* /*will have* problems with his teeth.

5 **A** Oh no. I'm going to be late for school again.
B No you're not. You *are* / *will be* on time if you *run* / *will run*.

6 **A** She *goes* / *will go* to the party if you *invite* / *will invite* her.
B Do you think so? I don't think she likes me very much.

■ **15** **Use the words to make questions.**

1 What / you do / rain / at the weekend?
What will you do if it rains at the weekend?

2 What programme / you watch / turn on the TV tonight?
....

3 What / you eat / feel hungry / after dinner tonight?
....

4 Where / you go / go away / this weekend?
....

5 What / you play / play sport / this weekend?
....

6 Who / you talk to / phone someone / tonight?
....

■ **16** **Write your answers to the questions in 15. Use your exercise book.**

▶ SB p. 51

Word File

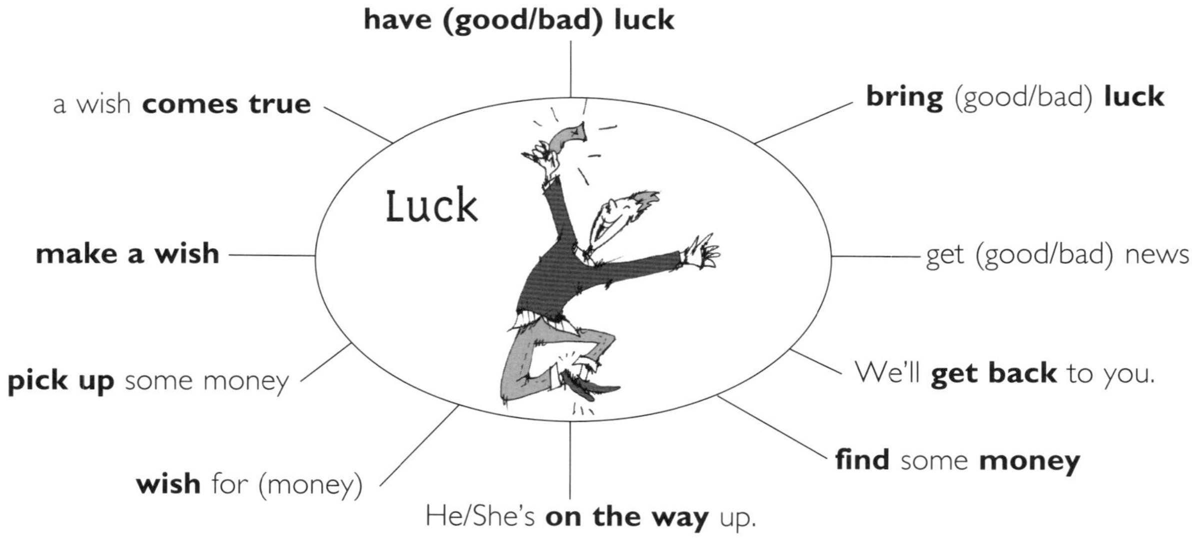

MORE Words and Phrases

■	1	**get out of** sb's way	*Get out of my way!*	jdm. aus dem Weg gehen
		see sb to the door	*I'll see you to the door.*	jdn. zur Tür begleiten
★	4	**discuss**	*Discuss what they saw and describe what happened.*	besprechen, diskutieren
●	5	block of flats	*In China, they leave a big hole in a block of flats so the ghosts can move through.*	Wohnblock
		hold sb **tight**(ly)	*In his dream, a snake was holding him tightly.*	jdn. festhalten
		magpie	*A magpie is a kind of bird.*	Elster
		superstition	*Believing something brings good or bad luck.*	Aberglaube
■	7	Anything else?	*Will there be anything else, sir?*	Sonst noch was?
		crack	*The cracks are the lines between the stones.*	Riss, Spalt; hier: Fuge
		cuckoo	*A cuckoo is a kind of bird.*	Kuckuck
		ladder	*You climb up a ladder to get to the roof.*	Leiter
		shake	*We shake hands when we meet people for the first time.*	schütteln
		superstitious	*Are you superstitious?*	abergläubisch
		turn round	*She turned round and went back home.*	(sich) umdrehen
■	9	**do** the dishes	*I'll do the dishes after dinner.*	(ab)spülen, abwaschen
★	10	**catch a cold**	*Take your jacket or you'll catch a cold.*	sich erkälten
		nonsense (no pl)	*I don't believe this nonsense.*	Unsinn, Quatsch

UNIT 7 You've got a friend!

Revision Vocabulary

● ① **Match the sentence halves.**

1 I can't tell you what I wished	☐ a wish. It's your birthday.
2 Go on. Make	☐ you seven year's bad luck.
3 Don't do that. It'll bring	☐ for. It's a secret.
4 My wish came	☐ luck. I don't.
5 Some people think that black cats bring good	☐ true. I met you!

● ② **Complete the sentences. There is one word missing.**

Grammar 1st Conditional

● ③ **Underline the correct option.**

1 If she *will find* / *<u>finds</u>* out, she *<u>will be</u>* / *is* angry.
2 If you *won't* / *don't* stop playing computer games, you *get* / *will get* a headache.
3 He *won't* / *doesn't* pass if he *won't* / *doesn't* study harder.
4 They *will phone* / *phone* us if they *will have* / *have* enough time.
5 We *will be* / *are* late if we *won't* / *don't* run.
6 That dog *stops* / *will stop* barking if you *give* / *will give* it some food.

■ ④ **Put the verbs in brackets into the correct tense.**

1 If you ......drive...... (drive) so fast, we ......will have...... (have) a crash.
2 If it .... (not rain) tomorrow, we .... (have) a picnic in the park.
3 Don't worry. I .... (buy) you a new one if I .... (break) it.
4 I .... (not tell) anyone if you .... (tell) me. I promise.
5 If he .... (read) this, he .... (understand) everything.
6 If she .... (not call), I .... (send) her a text.

END OF REVISION SECTION

5 Complete with the words in the box.

stud
like
business
take
terrible

Brenda What happened to your nose James? It looks ....
James It's my nose, not yours. Mind your own ....
Mark How long have you had that .... ?
James I've had it for a week. What do you think, Mark? Do you .... it?
Mark Sorry, I don't
Brenda I'm telling you as a friend, James. It doesn't look good – .... it out.

6 Complete the text. Write the correct word in each space.

Have you heard the news? James has *fallen* [1]...................... *with* Brenda. No, he hasn't *broken* [2]...................... *with* her because they weren't girlfriend and boyfriend – although I think she quite likes him. I say that because she really wants to [3] *make* .... *with* him. She even tried to say sorry. He wasn't interested. He's really angry with her. The problem started when she said that she didn't like his nose stud. He told her to [4]...................... *her own business.* I think that was a bit hard. But then she told him to take the stud out. Well, that made him really angry and he [5]...................... *out of* the room. He hasn't spoken to her for a week now. It's a pity because they were really good friends and *got* [6]...................... *really well* with each other.

1	up	out	through	4	take	do	mind
2	up	out	on	5	blew	rained	stormed
3	up	down	over	6	in	on	over

7 Match the phrases in italics above with their meanings.

1 to finish a romantic relationship ☐
2 don't give advice* to people if they don't ask you ☐
3 leave somewhere angrily ☐
4 have a good relationship with someone. ☐
5 stop talking to a friend ☐
6 become friends again ☐

VOCABULARY
***advice** – Ratschlag

8 Put the lines in order.

☐ **Jenny** Oh, that's easy. My laptop.
☐ **Jenny** Every day. I can't live without it.
☐ **Jenny** I've had it since last Christmas.
☐ **Interviewer** Your laptop? OK. How long have you had it?
1 **Interviewer** Hi, Jenny. Tell me, which of the things that you own do you like a lot?
☐ **Interviewer** And how often do you use it?

9 Now write your own dialogue.

▶ SB pp. 52, 53

■ 10 Read the conversation and complete the sentences.

Craig Have you read that article about young people and friendship?

Leonie No, I haven't.

Craig It's quite interesting. It tells you about things that are important to young people. And the most important thing is friendship.

Leonie I can believe that. So what do they say about it?

Craig Most young people only have a few really good friends. And then there are some they call friends, but they're not best friends, see?

Leonie Uh huh. Not like Tina and me. We've been best friends since we were little kids.

Craig Exactly. Best friends have known each other a long time. Many of them have been best friends since childhood. Even if they don't see each other for a long time, they're still best friends.

Leonie Uh huh. And what about the others?

Craig Well, they're just friends, you know. Like the people you hang out* with at weekends or you only meet at school.

Leonie What's the difference?

Craig Well, best friends tell each other everything. You don't tell other friends everything. And you can talk to your best friend about your problems. But with other friends you just have a good time and hang out.

Leonie But you also hang out with your best friends.

Craig Of course you do. But best friends know about your secrets and they help you out and stand by you*. And this is really, really important to young people.

Leonie That's true. So, Craig, we've known each other since were eight …

Craig And we've always been good friends. Does that make us best friends, too?

Leonie Of course it does!

1 The most important thing for young people is ....
2 Most young people only have a few ....
3 Tina and Leonie have been best friends since they ....
4 Best friends have known each other ....
5 With other friends, you hang out with them at ....
6 Best friends tell each other ....
7 With best friends you can talk about ....
8 Craig and Leonie have known each other since they ....

VOCABULARY
***hang out** – Zeit verbringen
***stand by sb** – zu jmd halten

■ 11 Complete the sentences with the correct form of the words in the box.

listen
borrow
lie
hear
keep
forget

My friends

1 Paul never .... my birthday and he always gets me a great present.
2 Lana's great. She can always .... a secret. I can tell her anything and she never tells anyone else.
3 Trevor never .... to a word I say. He only wants to talk about himself.
4 Kevin always says what I want to .... He makes me feel great.
5 Never let Sara .... anything. You'll never get it back.
6 Jane keeps .... to me. She never tells me the truth.

▶ SB pp. 53, 54

★ 12 **Read the story quickly. What colour is Wendy wearing at the end of it?**

Colour day

I got up in the morning and knew straightaway – it was a green day. I like green days. They are like springtime when the sun shines and the birds sing. People smile as they water the flowers on the balcony. I'm sure their eyes are green.

Anyway, it was a green day, so I put on my dark-green skirt and my light-green sweater. I spent half an hour putting on green nail-polish* and green eye-shadow.* I borrowed mum's green necklace (without asking) and went to school. I stopped at the shop for one of the nice green apples and I met a boy from the 4th form. His name is actually Henry Green. I don't usually talk to him, but today I said 'Hi, Henry', but he just looked at me. Stupid. Then I saw he had brown eyes and I was sorry for saying 'hi'. I went into my music class (1st lesson – maybe we'd sing The green, green grass of home) and saw a problem straightaway: I always sit next to Francine – and Francine was wearing a blue skirt and a white and orange blouse. I simply couldn't sit next to her! Nothing green about her at all. Not even her eyes. 'Sorry Francine,' I said. 'Today I feel like sitting all alone in the back row. I think I have a headache.' Francine didn't care. She was talking to Alan (all in black!) and just waved at me. So I sat down in the last row and felt a bit sad. Why didn't people understand it was a green day? I thought about giving a little presentation on colour days and how we should, maybe, decide with my expert help, on some colour days a year. But then I said no to my idea, because I could hear the others say: 'Weird Wendy' (that's my name). You see, I believe in colour days. Guess what happened next.

In walked our music teacher and behind her was a boy. A new boy, she said. His name was Nate – and he was wearing green jeans, a white and green T-shirt and green running shoes! The teacher looked around and then said: 'Why don't you sit next to Wendy, Nate? She can explain things to you.'

So Nate sat down and we got on well together right from the start! That was half a year ago and we've been friends ever since. But now I must hurry – my purple nail polish isn't dry yet, but Nate's waiting. I can see his purple cap outside the window.

VOCABULARY
***nail-polish** – Nagellack
***eye-shadow** – Lidschatten

▶ SB p. 54

■ **13** **Read the story again and answer the questions.**

What colour is/are:

1 Henry Green's eyes? ....
2 Wendy's sweater at the beginning of the story? ....
3 Alan's clothes? ....
4 the eyes of the people watering their flowers? ....
5 Nate's T-shirt? ....
6 Francine's blouse? ....
7 Nate's cap at the end of the story? ....
8 Francine's skirt? ....

★ **14** **Pick a colour. Then write a story about your colour day.**

Tip: Think of objects, clothes, buildings etc. but also of music or feelings that go well with your colour.

Grammar Present perfect

We've been students for years.

■ **15** **Complete with 'for' or 'since'.**

1 I have had my laptop .... half a year.
2 Molly has had her cat .... December.
3 Ben has had his piano .... he was six years old.
4 Mohammed has had his skateboard .... three months.

■ **16** **Use the prompts to write sentences.**

1 I / have / MP3 player / Christmas
I've had my MP3 player since Christmas.
2 I / have / laptop / six months.
3 My father / work / in that office / two years.
4 My sister / have / new dog / July.
5 They / live / in that flat / 2004.
6 You / have / this problem / two weeks.
7 I / not play / football / last year.
8 We / be / students at this school / a very long time!

■ **17** **Write 5 sentences that are true for you.**

I've had my sunglasses for four months.

I've had my	watch computer bike snowboard ear rings necklace MP3 player dog friendship band	for since	… months. … years. yesterday. Christmas. my birthday. last year. 2006. … weeks. … days.

■ **18** **Write three dialogues.**

How long has Dave had his sunglasses? – He's had them since his last birthday.

▶ SB p. **57**

Word File

MORE Words and Phrases

●	1	awful	*I think it looks awful.*	furchtbar, schrecklich, scheußlich
		for	*I haven't seen her for years.*	seit
		since	*I haven't spoken to her since then.*	seit
		stud	*Look, he's got a stud in his nose.*	Stecker, hier: Piercing
●	3	**go** to sleep	*I was very tired last night. I went to sleep at 9 o'clock.*	einschlafen
		soft toy	*I really like all the soft toys on my bed.*	Plüschtier, Kuscheltier
■	5	childhood (no pl)	*Childhood is the time when you are very young.*	Kindheit
		earring	*An earring is a kind of jewellery you can wear on*	Ohrring
		necklace	*A kind of jewellery you wear around your neck.*	Halskettte
■	6	**not either**	*I don't like you're haircut either.*	auch nicht
		haircut	*After your hair grows too long, you need a haircut.*	Haarschnitt, Frisur
		introduce	*I'd like to introduce you to my best friend.*	vorstellen
		in the meantime	*Our friends won't be here until later. In the meantime*	in der Zwischenzeit
		probably	*You're probably right – but I'm not sure.*	wahrscheinlich
		sulk	*You sulk when your friend hasn't called you for two*	sich erkälten
		understanding	*Try to be a bit more understanding.*	verständnisvoll
★	7	**interfere** (with sth)	*Do you sometimes interfere in other people's lives?*	sich (in etwas) einmischen
★	8	**beat sb**	*He beat me. He was better than me.*	jdn. besiegen
		judge	*A judge has to make sure that everything is correct.*	(Schieds-)Richter/in
★	13	**useful**	*Learn all these words! They will be useful.*	nützlich, brauchbar
	Fido	This is what friends are for!	*Thanks for helping. – No problem. This is what friends are for.*	Dafür sind Freunde da!

UNIT 8 Steven Spielberg superstar

Revision Vocabulary

1 Read the dialogue and match the phrases in italics with the phrases a) – f).

a) stormed out ☐
b) broke up with ☐
c) 've fallen out with ☐
d) make up ☐
e) mind your own business ☐
f) got on really well ☐

James [1] *I'm not talking to* Paul any more. I don't know why I thought he was my friend.
Olivia Oh, dear. What's happened?
James Well you know he [2] *stopped seeing* Jane about two weeks ago.
Olivia Yes, I remember. She wanted to try [3] *and start again with* him.
James That's right. But he wasn't interested.
Olivia So what's the problem?
James Well, Jane and I have always [4] *had a good relationship.*
Olivia No! You didn't?
James Well I didn't think there was a problem. He finished with her.
Olivia So did you tell him that Jane's your girlfriend now?
James Yes and he [5] *left the room really angrily.*
Olivia Well, of course he did. James, sometimes you are really stupid.
James And I think you should [6] *keep your opinions to yourself.* I love her.
Olivia I give up!

Grammar Present perfect

2 Complete with *for* or *since*.

1 She's been here ......for...... an hour.
2 She's been here .... 10 o'clock.
3 We've lived in this town .... 2003.
4 I've had my computer .... October.
5 He's been ill .... three days.
6 They've had their dog .... a month.
7 Mary's been in Paris .... last year.
8 We haven't eaten pizza .... two weeks.

3 Put the words into the correct order. Write the sentences.

1 my / had / computer / one / year / I've
I've had my computer for one year.
2 had / bike / a month / his / for / Tony's / new
....
3 sunglasses / had / last / weekend / Sue's / her / since
....
4 our / for / new / had / car / We've / a week
....
5 has / Christmas / had / He / since / dog / his
....

END OF REVISION SECTION

4 Read the first paragraph of the text on p. 58 of your Student's Book again and match the films with the descriptions.

1 *Jaws*
2 *Raiders of the Lost Ark*
3 *Jurassic Park*
4 *E.T.*
5 *Saving Private Ryan*
6 *Roger Rabbit, Pinky and the Brain* and *Shrek*
7 *War of the Worlds*

☐ People believed dinosaurs were alive.
☐ It was a war film.
☐ People didn't want to go swimming in the sea.
☐ They were funny.
☐ Lots of people wanted to be archaeologists.
☐ It made people cry.
☐ It had great special effects.

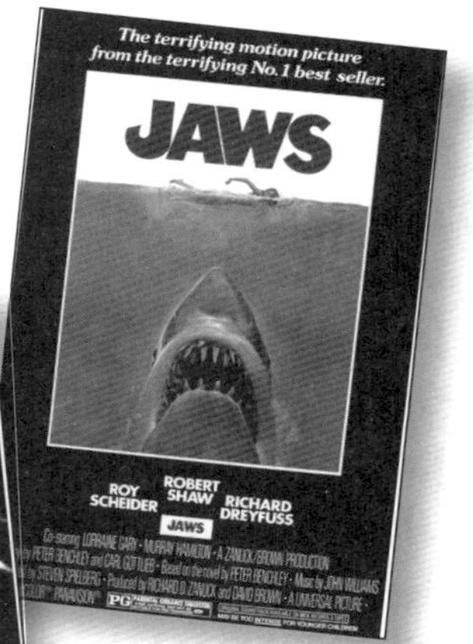

5 Read the second paragraph again and underline the correct options.

1 Spielberg is more than *60 / 80* years old.
2 He has produced *less / the same number of / more* films than he has directed.
3 He is not a *writer / an actor / a director.*
4 His first film was about *aliens / sharks / cowboys.*
5 It was *less than / more than / about* ten minutes long.
6 He made it in *1956 / 1958 / 1960.*
7 Other children *paid / didn't pay* to see his film.
8 His sister sold *tickets / food / drinks.*

6 Match the words with the pictures. Write the numbers in front of each word.

☐ western ☐ science fiction film ☐ horror film
☐ war film ☐ adventure film ☐ animated cartoon

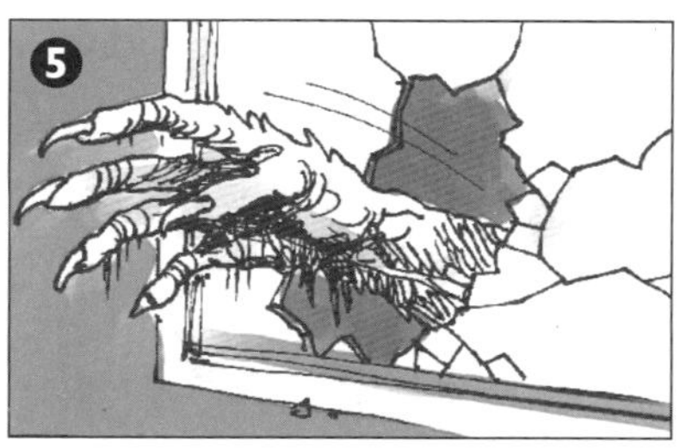

▶ SB pp. 58, 60

■ **7** **Read the text about monsters in the movies in your Student's Book again. Match each technique with three sentences to describe it.**

1 Stop-motion
2 Costumes
3 CGI

a) cinema audiences didn't believe it. ☐
b) invented by Ray. ☐
c) first seen in Jurassic Park. ☐
d) brought dinosaurs alive in the 50's. ☐
e) anything is now possible. ☐
f) used on actors and animals ☐
g) took a lot of time to do. ☐
h) cinema audiences believed it. ☐
i) a cheap idea from the 70's. ☐

● **8** **Complete the dialogue with the following phrases.**

What did you
lots of special effects
my favourite actor
Who's the director
Have you seen

Brian 1 .... any good films recently?
Annie Yeah, I saw *War of the Worlds.*
Brian 2 .... like about it?
Annie I think the actors were brilliant – especially Tom Cruise, of course. He's 3 ....
Brian 4 .... of *War of the Worlds?*
Annie Steven Spielberg, and that's why it's a very special film.
Brian Yeah, he is a great director. What's the story about?
Annie Well, it's about aliens coming to Earth. There are 5 .... They're really cool.
Brian Don't say any more! I want to see the film.

■ **9** **Underline the correct option to complete the sentences.**

1 Annie *didn't like / liked / loved* the actors in *War of the Worlds.*
2 Brian thinks Tom Cruise is *OK / good / the best.*
3 Steven Spielberg was the *director / producer / actor* in the film.
4 It's a *horror / science fiction / war film.*
5 Annie thought the film was *funny / scary / boring.*
6 Brian *hasn't seen / has seen / doesn't want to* see the film.

▶ SB pp. **59, 60**

■ **10 Put the dialogues in order.**

1 ☐ **A** So what was so good about it?
☐ **A** Did you cry?
[1] **A** What did you think of the film?
☐ **B** Everything. But I really loved the story. It was really moving.
☐ **B** It was brilliant.
☐ **B** Almost.

2 ☐ **A** But what?
[1] **A** Have you seen the new Tom Cruise film yet?
☐ **A** What! Are you crazy? He's the greatest actor in the world.
☐ **A** So? What did you think?
☐ **B** Not in this film, he wasn't.
☐ **B** Yes, I saw it last night.
☐ **B** I thought Tom Cruise wasn't very good.
☐ **B** Well, the special effects were awesome but …

■ **11 You've just seen a great film and you email your friend about it.**

Say:

- what it was
- why you liked it
- what was exciting/great/etc. about it
- what others thought of it
- why your friend should go and see it.

Grammar Present perfect and past simple

● **12 Match the questions and the answers.**

1 Have you ever been to Spain?
2 Has June finished her homework?
3 Have they found their cat?
4 Has he written you an email?
5 Have they found a new house?
6 Has the film started yet?

☐ Yes, she finished ten minutes ago.
☐ No, but he phoned me.
☐ Yes, and it's a very nice house.
☐ Yes, we went to Madrid last year.
☐ Yes, it started about 15 minutes ago.
☐ Yes, it was in the garden.

■ **13 Complete the sentences with present perfect or past simple.**

1 My sister ....got.......... married last Sunday. (get)
2 She .... her husband three years ago. (meet)
3 I .... a famous person in my life. (never meet)
4 Jacqueline's not very happy because she .... with her boyfriend. (just break up)
5 My team .... the cup final two–nil last night. (lose)
6 I'm sorry Robert's not in. He .... to the shops. (just go)
7 The flight from Belfast .... (already arrive)
8 The flight from Dublin .... more than an hour ago. (arrive)

▶ SB pp. **61, 65**

■ 14 Complete the dialogues with the correct forms of the words.

1 **A** .... you .... to Italy (be)?
B Yes, I .... (go) there last year.
A Which cities .... you .... (visit)?
B We .... (visit) Rome and Naples. We .... (have) a great time.

2 **A** .... you .... a famous person? (meet)
B Yes, I .... (meet) Bill Gates when I was 12.
A Wow. What .... you .... to him? (say)
B I .... (ask) him for some money.

■ 15 Write two more dialogues using these first lines.

1 Have you ever found a lot of money?
2 Have you ever had a bad accident?

■ 16 Fill in the past or the present perfect.

Chris Could I borrow some money from you?
Tom You still [1]............................... (not pay) back the money you [2]............................... (borrow) from me last week.
Chris What? I [3]............................... (not borrow) any money from you last week.
Tom Yes, you did. Remember? When you [4]............................... (buy) that new Keira Knightley DVD?
Chris Oh, yes. You're right. I [5]............................... (need) a present for Jenny.
Tom What? You [6]............................... (give) it to her? I [7]............................... (want) to watch it. It's all Jenny this, Jenny that. What about me?

Everyday English Bad hair day

Look at the phrases on p. 64 in your Student's Book again. Use them to complete the dialogues.

1 **A** Dad says he's going to buy a new television – maybe next month.
B .... This TV's useless!
2 **A** Jane, have you heard? You got top marks in the Maths test.
B ....
A No. I heard Mr Cooper telling someone and he's the Maths teacher, so he should know, shouldn't he?
3 **Dad** Jamie, please don't go out wearing those awful clothes!
Jamie Oh, Dad. .... These clothes are totally cool!
4 **A** OK. One more plate and then the washing-up's done!
B Well, ... We've still got to wash the glasses.

▶ SB p. 64

Word File

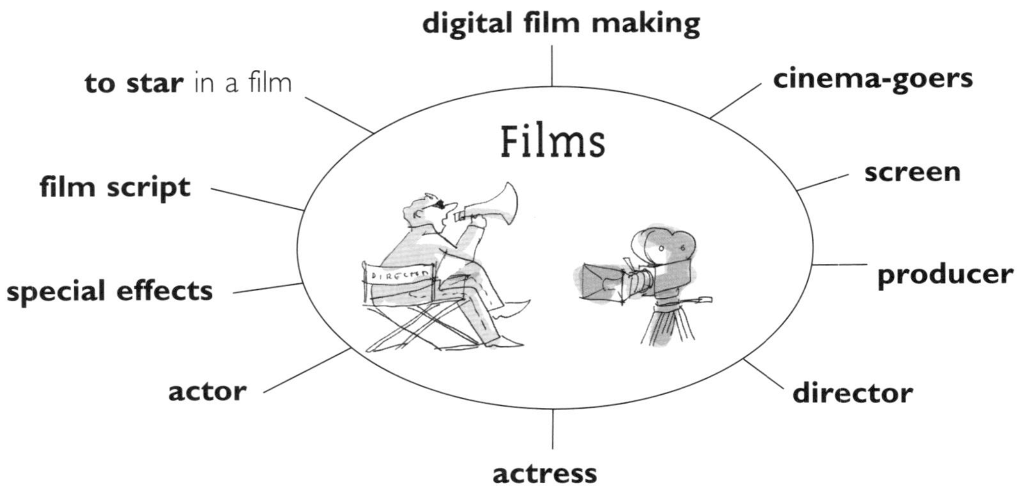

MORE Words and Phrases

■	1	**because of**	*People think Hollywood films are amazing because of one man: Steven Spielberg.*	wegen
		direct	*He has directed more than fifty films.*	leiten, führen; hier: Regie führen
		preparation	*The producer controls the preparation of a film.*	Vorbereitung
		successful	*Spielberg has always been successful.*	erfolgreich
		turn down (sb/sth)	*The film school turned him down twice.*	(jdn/etwas) ablehnen, abweisen
■	2	**develop**	*He developed the film script for 'Rain Man.'*	(sich) entwickeln
		success	*Her first real success as an actress was in 'Indiana Jones and the Temple of Doom.'*	Erfolg
★	3	**e.g.**	*The short form of "for example".*	z. B.
		rarely	*He rarely makes a bad film.*	selten, nicht oft
		surprise	*His films have always surprised us.*	überraschen
■	4	**research**	*The film is about a research centre.*	Forschung
		take a tour	*They took a tour of the park.*	an einer Fahrt teilnehmen
		be trapped	*Two children were trapped in a canteen. They couldn't get out.*	eingeschlossen sein
■	5	**a couple of**	*A couple of velociraptors were outside.*	einige, ein Paar
		feed	*The dinosaurs were feeding in the trees.*	fressen, weiden
		manage sth	*They managed to run away and get back to the visitor centre.*	etwas schaffen
		switch on/off	*They switched the electricity back on again.*	ein-/ausschalten
★	6	dress up	*You can dress up in a costume for Halloween.*	sich verkleiden
		generate	*Dinosaurs were generated with the help of computers.*	erzeugen
		image	*The images are generated for the film.*	Bild
★	7	**crowd**	*With the help of this technique you can create huge crowds of monsters.*	(Menschen)menge; Zuschauermenge
■	8	gripping	*This book is totally gripping.*	packend, fesselnd
●		moving	*It was a sad story and very moving.*	bewegend, ergreifend
	9	**recently**	*Have you seen any films recently?*	kürzlich, vor kurzem, neulich
★	13	**similar**	*Read this text and then write a similar one.*	ähnlich

UNIT 9 Young people today

Revision Vocabulary

● 1 **What kind of film do you think these are? Choose from the words in the box.**

thriller horror film animated cartoon adventure film western science fiction film

1 *They Came from Mars:* ....
2 *Dracula Lives Again:* ....
3 *Last Cowboy in Dodge City:* ....
4 *The Search for King Solomon's Gold:* ....
4 *Inspector Butler's Last Case:* ....
6 *The Simpsons:* ....

● 2 **What do you think about these types of films? Write a sentence for each one.**

'I usually like horror films, but I don't like them if they are too scary.'

1 ....
2 ....
3 ....
4 ....
5 ....
6 ....

Grammar Present perfect and past simple

● 3 **Underline the correct option.**

1 I *spoke / have spoken* to Tom yesterday.
2 I *didn't speak / haven't spoken* to Tom yet.
3 *Did you ever eat / Have you ever eaten* octopus?
4 You can't be hungry. You *ate / have eaten* three pizzas for lunch.
5 We *never went / have never been* to the USA in our life.
6 We *went / have been* to California last year.

■ 4 **Complete the sentences with past simple or present perfect.**

1 I'm sorry June isn't here. She .... (leave) ten minutes ago.
2 We .... (play) really badly last week. I'm not surprised we lost!
3 Where's Anna this morning? She .... (not speak) to me for three days.
4 They .... (not be) to London before.
5 .... you .... (enjoy) the party last night?
6 I .... (live) here since May.

END OF REVISION SECTION

5 **Read the text on p. 69 of your Student's Book and put the following points in the order that Curtis talks about them.**

- [ ] his room
- [ ] what he does in the winter
- [ ] things he has to do around the house
- [ ] what his parents do
- [ ] an adventure last year

6 **Write a few sentences for each of the points in 5.**

1 *His room is quite big. He has got a PC, a stereo and a TV in it.*
2 ....
3 ....
4 ....
5 ....

7 **Split the word snake into 16 activities.**

dyeyourhairgetatattoogorollerskatingwithoutpadsbuyyourownclotheshaveapartyathomeuseyourparents'camcordergotothediscocomehomeaftertenattheweekendturnyourmusicupreallyloudgetanosestudplayvideogamesalldaywatchTVafteroo'clockeattoomanysweets

8 **Which of the activities above are these people doing?**

They're having a party at home.
....
....
....
....
....
....
....
....
....
....
....
....

▶ SB pp. 69, 71

9 Match the questions and answers.

1 Are you allowed to invite your friends over?
2 Are you allowed to come home late?
3 Are you allowed to get your hair dyed?
4 Are you allowed to get a tattoo?
5 Are you allowed to surf the internet?
6 Are you allowed to have a pet at home?

- [ ] Maybe if I choose a nice colour.
- [ ] Yes, but I'm not allowed to go into chat rooms.
- [ ] No, because my dad's allergic to animals.
- [ ] Yes, but I have to be back by 9 p.m. on week nights.
- [ ] Yes but we're not allowed to make too much noise.
- [ ] No. My dad would kill me.

10 Write your own answers to the questions.

11 Read about these children. Which South American countries are they from? Write the names of the countries below the texts.

Venezuela Bolivia Brazil Peru

My name is José. Every weekend I help my father to water corn plants in a field in the desert. The field belongs to the government. My parents can buy the land if they grow something. So every weekend we take water to the field because there is not much rain here. My sister can't come – she's eighteen and she works in the capital city, Lima. It's a long way from here.

....

My name is Agripina. I live high up in the mountains. It's beautiful here. From our little house I can see the Illimani. And at night I can see the lights of La Paz. Every day after school I go and look after our animals. We have 16 alpacas. They are very important for us because once a year we sell their wool.

....

My name is Renato. I live on the east coast of the biggest country of South America. There is a beautiful beach near our village and I go surfing almost every day. There is one problem. Every morning my friends and I find lots of plastic bottles, plastic bags and other stuff on the beach. We think that people on big ships throw the stuff into the sea. It makes us very angry.

....

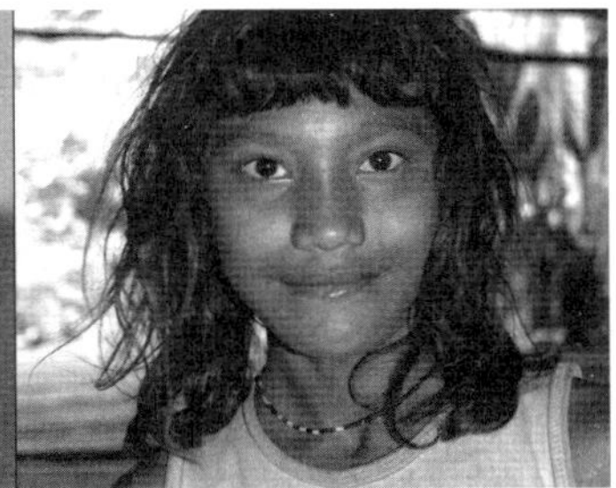

My name is Raukani. Our tribe are the Warao. I live with my parents and my two brothers and three sisters on the Orinoco river. There are no cars here or motorbikes. When we go on a trip we use the canoe. Our children learn to use it before they can walk. There is no school here. I learn everything from my parents.

....

12 Read again and answer the questions. Write Raukani, Renato, Agripina or José.

1 Who doesn't go to school? ....
2 Who lives at a high altitude? ....
3 Who helps his father grow things to eat? ....
4 Who likes water sports? ....
5 Who travels by water? ....
6 Who gets angry about pollution*? ....
7 Who doesn't live with his sister? ....
8 Who looks after animals? ....

VOCABULARY
***pollution** – Umweltverschmutzung

▶ SB pp. **72, 73**

■ **13** **Read the text about 14-year-old Australian teenager.**

Australian adventures

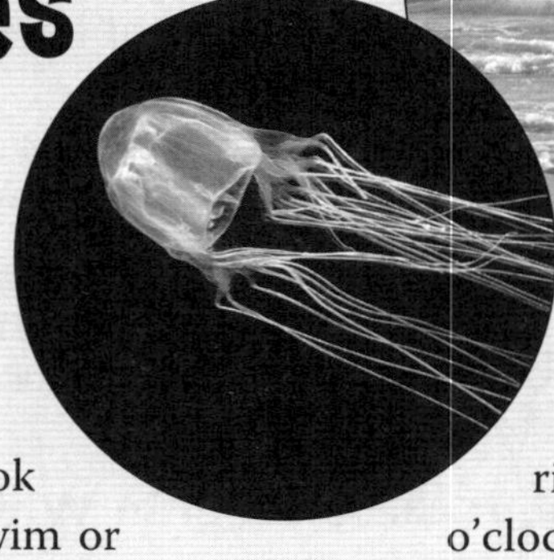

Hi, my name's Brett. My family, that's mum, dad and me, live in Broome, Western Australia. Western Australia is about 80 times larger than Italy, but only 1,5 million people live there. Broome is in the north of Western Australia. It's a town with a population of about 12,000. Broome is right on the coast and its known for its famous Cable Beach, which is 20km long. Both my parents work. My father is a mechanic and my mother is a nurse*. We live in a bungalow with a large garden. I often help my father at the weekends when he repairs* cars for friends. When we drive out into the bush, dad often lets me drive. Of course, I am not allowed to drive in town.

At the weekends I often go fishing or swimming with my friends or my parents. We drive to Cable Beach and look for a quiet place to swim or to fish. From October to March we do not go swimming because there may be box jellyfish in the water. The box jellyfish is one of the most deadly jellyfish. In Australia, they kill up to 65 people a year. If they sting you, the best thing to do is to put vinegar* over the skin. That's why we always take a bottle of vinegar with us.

Another dangerous animal in Western Australia is the saltwater crocodile. A year ago I went camping in the bush with my friend Shaun and his dad. We wanted to do some fishing and set up camp about 20 metres from a river. Suddenly at 3 o'clock in the morning we felt something pulling on our tent. We were very scared. Shaun's father turned the torch on and we quickly got out of the tent* and ran to the car which was parked close. Shaun's dad started the car and in the headlights* we could see a big crocodile that was pulling the tent into the river. We were so shocked that we drove straight home. We had to drive all night and when we arrived in Broome in the morning we told the police about the crocodile attack.

VOCABULARY
***nurse** – Krankenschwester
***repair** – reparieren
***vinegar** – Essig
***tent** – Zelt
***headlights** – Scheinwerferlicht

■ **14** **Tick the correct answer.**

1 The boy's name is
a) ☐ Shaun. b) ☐ Brett. c) ☐ Broome.

2 He and his parents live in
a) ☐ a house. b) ☐ a boat. c) ☐ a flat.

3 In Broome there are about
a) ☐ 1,5 million people.
b) ☐ 1200.
c) ☐ 12,000.

4 Western Australia is about
a) ☐ 80.
b) ☐ 18.
c) ☐ 8 times bigger than Italy.

5 Swimming in Broome is dangerous
a) ☐ from October to March.
b) ☐ from March to October.
c) ☐ in March.

6 When a jellyfish has stung you should pour vinegar
a) ☐ on the skin.
b) ☐ on the jellyfish.
c) ☐ into the water.

7 On a camping holiday a crocodile attacked
a) ☐ their car. b) ☐ the tent. c) ☐ the police.

8 After the attack they drove straight
a) ☐ home. b) ☐ to a hotel. c) ☐ to the police.

★ **15** **Get in touch with a friend/a relative. Ask him/her about their daily life and write a short report.**

GRAMMAR *be allowed to*

■ **16** **Put the dialogue in order.**

☐ **A** Yes, Fridays and Saturdays too.
[1] **A** Are you allowed to come home late?
☐ **A** I have to be home by 10 p.m. every night.
☐ **B** Yes, but only at the weekends. What about you?
☐ **B** Wow. Your parents are strict.
☐ **B** What! Even on Saturdays?

■ **17** **Write similar dialogues for the questions below. Use your exercise book.**

1 Are you allowed to borrow your dad's camcorder?
2 Are you allowed to buy your own clothes?

■ **18** **Match the signs and the sentences.**

☐ A You aren't allowed to park here.
☐ B You aren't allowed to swim here.
☐ C You aren't allowed to walk on the grass.
☐ D You aren't allowed to go in here.
☐ E You aren't allowed to eat food in here.
☐ F You aren't allowed to take photographs.

★ **19** **Fill in the correct forms of *be allowed* to.**

'On the school trip, you [1]................................ (not allow) to stay up later than 10 o'clock,' our teacher said. 'And you [2]................................ (not allow) to get together in one room and make a lot of noise.' That was before the trip, but during the trip it was even worse. We [3].. (not allow) to use our mobile phones for games and we [4].. (not allow) to listen to music during meals. 'Is there anything we [5]................................ (allow) to do?' I asked the teacher. 'I'll think about it,' he said. 'Ask me again next week.' I think teachers like that shouldn't [6]................................ (allow) to go on school trips.

■ **20** **Write sentences using the correct form of *be allowed to*.**

1 James ✓ watch TV / ✗ not watch TV after 10 o'clock.
James is allowed to watch TV, but he isn't allowed to watch TV after 10 o'clock.

2 Sarah ✓ go to bed late / ✗ not get up late.
....

3 We ✓ wear jeans to school / ✗ not wear shorts.
....

4 They ✓ listen to music / ✗ not listen without headphones.
....

5 I ✓ go to my friend's house / ✗ not stay overnight.
....

6 She ✓ have parties at home / ✗ not play loud music.
....

▶ SB p. 75

Word File

Teen activities

- **to come home** after ten at the weekend
- **to go** roller skating without pads
- **to buy** your own clothes
- **to go** to the disco
- **to turn** your music **up** really loud
- **to dye** your hair
- **to eat** too many sweets
- **to use** your parents' camcorder
- **to watch** TV after 10 o'clock
- **to play** video games all day
- **to hang out** in shopping centres
- **to get** a tattoo
- **to wear** earrings
- **to ride** your bike without a helmet
- **to have** a party at home

MORE Words and Phrases

●	1	**do** the cleaning	*Milase's mother does the cleaning for a rich family.*	sauber machen, putzen
		clear the snow	*In winter you have to clear the snow in front of your house.*	Schnee räumen
		dentist	*A dentist looks after your teeth.*	Zahnarzt/Zahnärztin
		grizzly bear	*A grizzly bear is the biggest and strongest bear in America.*	Grizzlybär
		grow sth	*We want to grow vegetables next summer.*	etwas anbauen, wachsen lassen
		housewife (pl housewives)	*Her mother looks after their home. She is a housewife.*	Hausfrau
		housework	*I don't have to do any housework.*	Hausarbeit
		royal	*The queen is the head of the British royal family.*	königlich
■	3	military service	*The Mennonites don't take part in the military service.*	Militärdienst
		movement	*The Mennonite movement began in the 16th century.*	Bewegung
■	4	**border**	*We crossed the border from Mexico.*	Grenze
		go ahead	*Yes, of course you can. Go ahead!*	fortfahren, weitermachen
		high school	*In America, after primary school you go to high school.*	Gymnasium
		strict	*Some parents are really strict about going out late.*	streng
		You're **welcome.**	*Thanks a lot. – You're welcome!*	Keine Ursache, Gern geschehen
●	6	fake	*It's not real, it's fake.*	falsch, gefälscht
■	11	**attention**	*Pay attention in class!*	Aufmerksamkeit

UNIT 10 Stand up for your rights

Revision Vocabulary

■ **1 Complete the poem with the missing verbs.**

The Rebel

rides, watches, going, loves, got, washed, got, dyed, have, has, turns, hangs, eats, are

He's [1]........................ a nose stud.
He's [2]........................ his hair blue.
He [3]........................ his motorbike
And he's [4]........................ a tattoo.

He [5]........................ parties at home
When his parents [6]........................ away.
He [7]........................ the music up loud
And [8]........................ TV all day.

He [9]........................ his bike with no helmet.
He [10]........................ too many sweets.
He [11]........................ out in department stores.
He hasn't [12]........................ for weeks.

He's [13]........................ to the disco
Tonight to [14]........................ some fun.
Tomorrow's his birthday.
He's going to be forty-one.

Grammar *be allowed to*

■ **2 Match the questions and answers.**

1 Why don't you wear jeans to school?
2 Why weren't you at the party?
3 Why don't you take your mobile phone to school?
4 Why isn't there a TV in your bedroom?
5 Why are you leaving the party so soon?
6 Do you want one of my puppies?

☐ I wasn't allowed to go.
☐ We're not allowed to use them there.
☐ I'm not allowed to have one.
☐ We're not allowed to wear them.
☐ No thanks. I'm not allowed a pet.
☐ I'm not allowed to stay out too late.

■ **3 Write sentences about these people.**

1

Jack isn't allowed to play football.

2

....

3

....

4

....

5

....

6

....

END OF REVISION SECTION

● 4 Match the sentence halves.

1 We need to organise
2 We're going
3 If you're free on Friday, can you help us hand
4 Have you thought about sending

☐ a meeting to see how people feel about this.
☐ out leaflets in the high street?
☐ out emails telling people about the problem?
☐ on a protest march against the war tomorrow.

■ 5 Put the dialogue in order.

☐ **A** Exactly. Work's going to start next month. That's why I need you to help me.
☐ **A** We want to start a petition and hand out leaflets to all the people in the village.
☐ **A** Will you help us?
[1] **A** They're planning to build a motorway through our village.
☐ **B** That's a brilliant idea.
☐ **B** Through the village? That's stupid!
☐ **B** Help you with what?
☐ **B** Of course.

■ 6 Choose one of the situations below and write a short dialogue. Use the dialogue above to help you.

There are plans to build a supermarket where the tennis courts are.

The school library is not open any more in the afternoon.

Children are not allowed to use school computers for their project work.

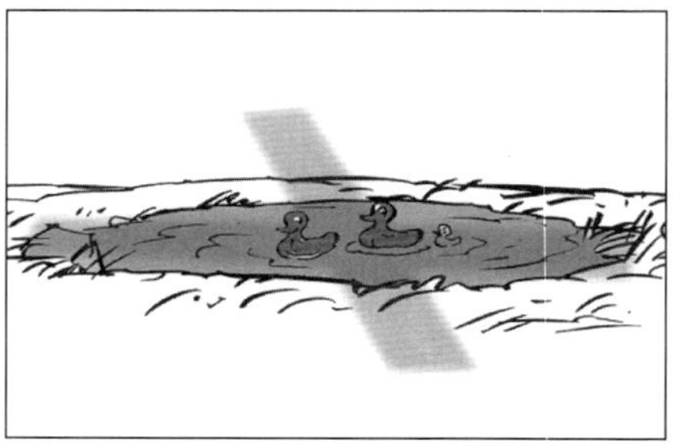

They want to remove the pond in the park.

■ 7 Look at the words in the box and complete the sentences.

distances
plastic bags
recycle
locally produced
litter bugs
save

1 It is very important to .... water.
2 You should really buy .... food.
3 I never take .... at my food store.
4 We always .... glass bottles and take them to the bottle bank.
5 Only .... leave bottles and cans on the beach.
6 People shouldn't drive short .... , they should use their bikes or walk.

▶ SB p. 78

■ **8** **Look at the pictures. Write sentences about what these people should/shouldn't do.**

He should buy locally produced apples. ……………… ………………

……………… ……………… ………………

● **9** **Write sentences that are true for you.**

Example: *I never ask my parents to drive me short distances.*

1 ………………
2 ………………
3 ………………
4 ………………

■ **10** **Read the dialogue and complete with the phrases in the box.**

stick to the rules
organise a protest
should talk
promise
last year
unfair

Karen Did you hear about the end-of-school-year party?

Julian No, what is it?

Karen The head* said we won't be allowed to have one.

Julian But that's [1]……………… . There's always been one. Why did he say that?

Karen He said that some boys were drinking alcohol [2]……………… and that some troublemakers* turned up in the evening.

Julian What's that got to do with us?

Karen He said pupils had to behave and [3]……………… . If they don't, they can't have a party.

Julian Listen, I know that, but that was last year. I think we [4]……………… to him again.

Karen That's what my mum said, too. She said we should go through the rules with the head again and we should [5]……………… to keep them.

Julian And if he says no?

Karen Then we can [6]……………… at school, can't we? My brother told me they organised one four years ago about the sports field and it worked.

Julian Okay, let's do that.

VOCABULARY
***head** – Schulleiter/in ***troublemakers** – Unruhestifter

▶ SB p. 78

■ 11 Write answers to the questions.

1 What was the problem with the party?
2 What happened last year?
3 What did the head want the students to do?
4 What suggestion does Julian make?
5 What suggestion does Karen's mum make?
6 What are they planning to do if the head says no?

■ 12 Read the letter to the headmaster and find 4 differences from the dialogue.

Dear Mr Richards,

We are writing to ask you to think again about the end-of-year party. As you know, this is a very popular event. All the school leavers* love it. We understand that last year there was some trouble and some of the boys did not behave very well. We know that three windows were broken and we understand that you don't want this to happen again. But you don't have to stop our party. That was last year's school leavers, not us. We are asking you to change your mind, please.

If you say that we can't have our party, then we will have to organise a protest march. We are sure that all the students in all the years will join. Please remember that two years ago my brother organised a protest about the school library and it worked. We are sure that you don't want something like that to happen again.

Thank you for your attention.

Karen Harvey

VOCABULARY
***leaver** – Abgänger(in)

★ 13 Look at the following notice. Then write a letter to the head teacher asking him/her to re-open the lab.

VOCABULARY
***until further notice** – bis auf Weiteres

Unfortunately, many students have not stuck to the rules for the computer lab, such as: not taking food in, not endlessly surfing the net, not printing out too many pages, etc. Therefore, the lab is closed until further notice*.

....

....

....

....

....

....

▶ SB p. 78

GRAMMAR *be able to*

■ **14 Underline the correct form of *be able to*.**

1 I *won't be able / wasn't able* to do my homework tonight. I haven't got time.
2 He spoke so fast. I *won't be able / wasn't able* to understand anything he said.
3 They got the visa. They *were able / will be able* to visit us next month.
5 She *was able / has been able* to stop the man and the police arrested him last night.
6 We *won't be able / weren't able* to come to your party next Friday. I'm sorry.
7 We *weren't able / won't be able* to go to the cinema because we didn't have enough money.
8 I'm sorry I *wasn't able / haven't been able* to write to you for such a long time.

● **15 Look at what happened yesterday. Write the children's names under the pictures.**

Yesterday …

1 Jill couldn't go to school.
2 Joanna wasn't able to buy the dress.
3 James couldn't phone his friend.
4 Sue wasn't able to get into the garden.
5 Lucy and Andy couldn't ride their bikes.
6 Mark and Ron weren't able to play.

....

....

....

....

....

....

■ **16 Write 6 sentences. What are the children's hopes for tomorrow?**

Tomorrow …

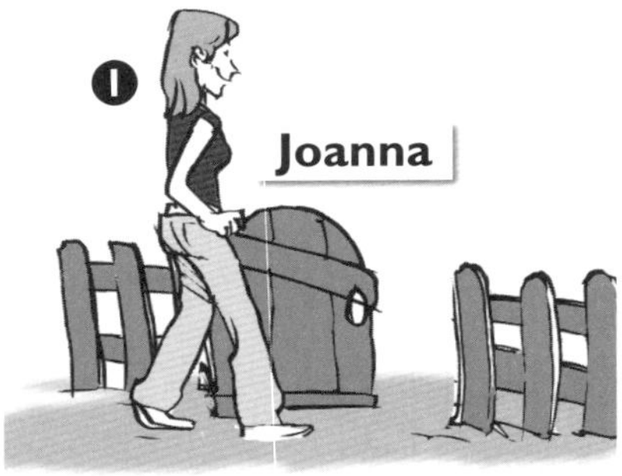

Jill *I'll be able to go to school.* ....

....

....

....

....

....

Everyday English Girls and football

Look at the phrases on p. 82 in your Student's Book again.
Use them to complete the dialogues.

1 **A** .... Steve's going out with Julie now.
B .... He was always looking at her.

2 **A** My dad's bought a Harley Davidson motorbike.
B .... ! Can we go for a ride on it?
A .... ! He won't even take me out on it, so he certainly won't take you!

▶ SB pp. **82, 83**

Word File

Getting the message across

to **sign a petition**
to **go on a protest march**
to **send out e-mails**
to **hand out leaflets**
to **organise a meeting**

Being green

to **save water**
to **buy locally produced food**
to **recycle** (glass bottles)
Don't **take plastic bags** at your food store.
Don't **drop litter**.
Don't **leave** bottles or cans in the park.
Don't **drive short distances**.

MORE Words and Phrases

		right(s)	*Stand up for your rights!*	Recht(e)
■	2	**be able to do**	*Our kids won't be able to play here.*	tun können
		chairman (pl chairmen)	*The chairman is the leader of the council.*	Vorsitzende/r; Vorstand
		come up with a **solution**	*It's sometimes difficult to come up with a solution that*	eine Lösung finden
		playing field	*There's no playing field in the park.*	Sportplatz
		headline	*In a newspaper, do you only read the headlines?*	Schlagzeile
		multi-storey car park	*The playing field is being changed into a multi-storey car park.*	(mehrstöckiges) Parkhaus
■	3	**against**	*Some kids are against the idea.*	gegen
■	4	city council	*Let's write e-mails to city council.*	Stadtrat
		How about …?	*How about signing a petition?*	Wir wäre es mit …?
		the latest	*Here's the latest!*	der/die/das jüngste/letzte; hier: das Neueste
		traffic lights	*Traffic lights control how fast cars can move in a town*	Ampel
■	8	**at least**	*You should at least try.*	wenigstens
		bottle bank	*We take all our old bottles to the local bottle bank.*	Altglascontainer
		container	*Put paper into special containers to be recycled.*	Behälter
		hardly (ever)	*I hardly ever eat meat.*	kaum
		litter bug	*Keep things tidy. Don't be a litter bug!*	Umweltverschmutzer/in
		wrapping	*Don't ever throw wrappings into the street.*	Verpackung
★	9	suffragette	*The suffragettes wanted the right to vote for women.*	Frauenrechtlerin
		vote	*They fought for the right to vote.*	wählen
★	10	**arrest**	*One way to escape arrest is to go abroad.*	Verhaftung
		reader	*As our readers know, we write about suffragettes.*	Leser/in
		vote	*Are you going to go to the vote on Sunday?*	Abstimmung, Wahl
■	11	**decision**	*She made the right decision.*	Entscheidung
		democracy	*In a democracy, people vote for their political leaders.*	Demokratie
		environment	*You can save water to protect the environment.*	Umgebung; hier: Umwelt
		refuse	*Rosa Parks refused to give up her seat on a bus to a white man.*	ablehnen

UNIT 11 California Dreaming

Revision Vocabulary

1 Complete the dialogue with the words in the box.

recycle
hand
sent
sign
protest
save

Anita Will you [1]................................. my petition?
Jeff Maybe. What's it about?
Anita We're asking the local council to [2]................................. paper and bottles. We're trying to [3]................................. the environment!
Jeff Well, that's a great idea. But a petition won't work. You need to go on a [4]................................. march.
Anita No, we don't want to do that. We [5]................................. out emails to lots of people – they all thought a petition was the best idea.
Jeff Well, OK. But petitions don't really help! Why don't you [6]................................. out leaflets?
Anita Because leaflets cost money and we haven't got any money!
Jeff Hmm – I see what you mean. OK – let me see the petition.

Grammar *could(n't) and (not) be able to*

2 Match sentences and pictures.

1 We couldn't get it down.
2 We couldn't understand him.
3 She hasn't been able to go to school.
4 'Will you be able to fix it?'
5 'Sorry, I won't be able to play tomorrow.'
6 'I don't think we'll be able to go to the beach this afternoon.'

3 Write the correct forms of '(not) be able to'.

1 My computer broke, so I .... check my emails last night.
2 We played well last Sunday, but the other team played better so we .... beat them.
3 My parents .... go to London at the weekend because Dad had to work on Saturday.
4 If I study hard, I think I .... pass next week's test.
5 I'm having a party next Saturday – I hope you .... come.
6 I've lost my mobile phone, so I .... phone anyone since yesterday.

END OF REVISION SECTION

■ ④ Read the text about California and mark the statements T (*True*) or F (*False*).

California

– Warm and Friendly

Why do millions of visitors go to California every year? The sun and the sand? The mountains and the valleys? The cities? We asked some tourists why they were here. This is what we found out.

Some of the biggest attractions of the Golden State are the cities. In fact, many tourists don't go any further than San Francisco and Los Angeles. Carl from Germany said that they were two of the best cities in the world: 'They've got everything that tourists are looking for', he said. But not all tourists are only interested in the big cities. The smaller towns are also very popular. June Woo Kim from South Korea said she enjoyed walking around towns like Monterey and Carmel because they were great for shopping.

The famous beach towns also have a lot of fans, especially among the younger visitors. Shaun and Debbie from Australia think that Santa Monica, Santa Cruz and Santa Barbara have got great beaches and that they're as good as the beaches in Australia.

Other things that our tourists liked about California included the great natural sights such as Yosemite National Park and the Big Sur, the museums and other attractions.

But everyone agreed on one thing: Californian people give a warm, friendly welcome to their visitors. And Donna and Brian from England were not the only people who told us that they loved the Californian people because they were so friendly. When we asked them if they plan to visit again, they said they're going to come back next year!

		T	F
1	The magazine only interviewed people from Germany.	☐	☐
2	California is known as the Golden State.	☐	☐
3	A lot of tourists only stay in the big cities.	☐	☐
4	June Woo Kim likes shopping.	☐	☐
5	A lot of young people go to the beach towns.	☐	☐
6	Shaun and Debbie said the beaches were better in Australia.	☐	☐
7	Some people think the Californians are a bit unfriendly.	☐	☐
8	Donna and Brian are going to Florida next year.	☐	☐

■ ⑤ Read the text again and …

a make a list of things that tourists to California find attractive.
b make a list of towns and cities in California.
c make a list of natural attractions in California.

■ ⑥ Use information from ⑤ and complete the dialogue with your own ideas.

1 **Fred** I'm going to California next month. Which towns and cities should I visit?
You Well, I think ....
....
....

2 **Angela** I really love nature and I'm going to California. What are the best places for me to visit?
You I think ....
....
....

▶ SB p. 86

7 Match the sentences.

1 The beaches in Santa Barbara are fantastic.
2 The mountains in Yosemite National Park are amazing.
3 San Francisco is great.
4 California is a very friendly place.
5 Santa Cruz is a cool city.
6 You should try some Californian grapes.

☐ It's an amazing city and there's always something to do there.
☐ There's always a big welcome waiting there for you.
☐ They're delicious*.
☐ They're really clean and the sand is beautiful.
☐ It's got some great beaches.
☐ They're so high.

VOCABULARY
***delicious** – köstlich

8 Think of three places that you know well. Write sentences about them. Give your opinion and explain it.

Examples:
London is a bit boring. It always rains there.
Vienna's a great city. There's lots of things to do there.

1 ....
....
2 ....
....
3 ....
....

9 Complete the dialogues with the words in the box.

dry
signal
spot
backpack
headquarters
dirt

1 **A** We're in trouble! Call your parents on your mobile phone.
B I can't! There's no .... here!

2 **A** Look at this photo. Do you know what this building is?
B Yes, it's the United Nations .... in New York.

3 **A** How do you carry things when you're cycling?
B I put everything in my ....

4 **A** Do you like cycling?
B Yes, but not in the city – I like to go to the mountains and cycle on .... roads.

5 **A** I was at the match yesterday, too.
B I know – but there were so many people there, I couldn't .... you in the crowd.

6 **A** Why don't you wear your jeans?
B Because I washed them this morning and they aren't .... yet.

▶ SB pp. **87, 88**

■ **10** **Put the dialogue in the correct order.**

- ☐ **A** Oh, I know – the Golden Gate Bridge!
- 1 **A** How long have you been living in San Francisco, Billy?
- ☐ **A** Oh? Is Oakland in California too?
- ☐ **A** How far away is it?
- ☐ **B** Yes, it's near San Francisco.
- ☐ **B** Well, we don't actually live in San Francisco. We live in Oakland.
- ☐ **B** Well, no – it's another bridge, called the Bay Bridge.
- ☐ **B** Not far. But you have to go over a bridge to get there.

■ **11** **Complete the crossword about California. All the information is in Unit 11 in the Student's Book.**

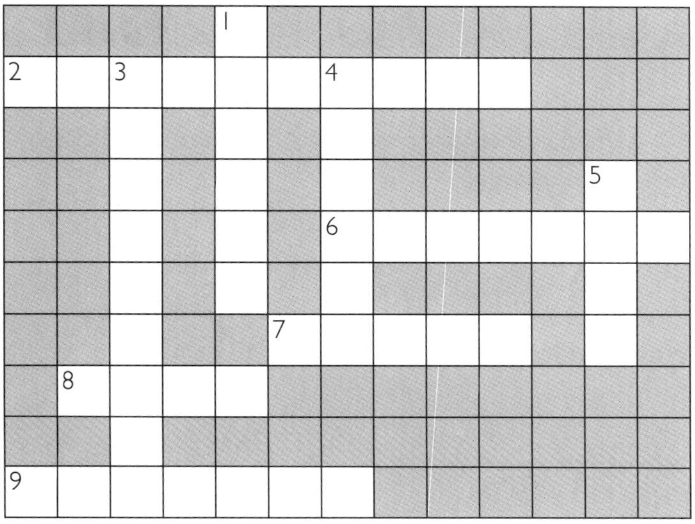

1 Lots of people go skateboarding at … Beach.
2 … is a big Disney park at Anaheim.
3 At The California Adventure, there's a ride called 'California …'
4 … was a dog that became famous in Hollywood films.
5 In the 19th century, many people went to California to try to find …
6 In Hollywood, you can visit Universal …
7 In … Valley, the temperature is sometimes 50°.
8 There's a lot of … in the Napa Valley.
9 Los … is the biggest city in California, but it isn't the capital.

■ **12** **Choose a place in California that you like. Imagine you are on holiday there. Write a postcard to an English-speaking friend.**

★ **13** **Look at the picture and read the introduction. Then write a short story in your exercise book and give it a title.**

The sun was hot. The water was cold. And the people were perfect. Almost too perfect. Everybody was fit and smiling. Maybe too fit. And maybe smiling too much. And there I was. An ordinary guy …

▶ SB pp. **86, 88**

GRAMMAR Present perfect continuous

■ **14 Match the sentences and the pictures.**

1 They look tired. They've been running for three hours.
2 He's been watching TV all night.
3 She's been waiting for twenty minutes.
4 He's been talking on his mobile for an hour.
5 They've been practising this song for a long time.
6 She's been dreaming of a new mountain bike for months.
7 You've been chasing cats again!
8 He's only been playing for a month.

■ **15 Put the words in the correct order and write the sentences.**

1 raining / all day / has been / It.

....

2 have been / I / presents / for / shopping.

....

3 He / two months / has been / for / as a waiter / working.

....

4 April / has been / She / the two children / since / looking after.

....

5 have been / They / in the doctor's waiting room / sitting / for an hour.

....

6 have been / three days / We / for the test / for / studying.

....

■ **16 Put the verbs in brackets into the correct form of the present perfect continuous.**

1 **A** Why are you so tired?
B I .... very hard. (work)

2 **A** Please get off the phone! You .... for almost an hour! (talk)
B Sorry! Here you are.

3 **A** Are you angry with me?
B Yes, I am! I .... for you for an hour! (wait)

4 **A** You play the piano very well.
B Yes. I .... lessons for three years. (take)

5 **A** How long .... you .... English? (learn)
B For about two years.

6 **A** .... you .... in this house for a long time? (live)
B Yes – since I was born.

▶ SB p. 72

Word File

A holiday in Death Valley

- a **dry** place
- to **have no signal**
- a **dirt road**
- a **backpack**
- **to spot** something
- a **mountain range**
- a **canyon**
- a **ridge**
- a **valley**
- **headquarters**

MORE Words and Phrases

●	1	**rent** sth	*We rented a jeep in San Jose.*	etwas mieten
■	3	**wine**	*They make good wine in California, too.*	Wein
■	4	**climate**	*I really like the climate in California.*	Klima
★	5	four-wheel-drive	*We need a jeep with four-wheel-drive in the desert.*	mit Allradantrieb
		gold digger	*Gold diggers were the people trying to find gold.*	Goldgräber
		gold rush	*The California gold rush began in 1849.*	Goldrausch
		on top	*Soon we were on top of a ridge.*	oben; obenauf
		shade (no pl)	*I stayed in the shade of a giant rock.*	Schatten
		sights (pl)	*We looked at all the sights in Los Angeles.*	Sehenswürdigkeiten
		be situated	*Where is Death Valley situated?*	liegen
		steep	*A canyon is a valley with steep sides of rock.*	steil
		take a photo	*He wanted to take photos in the mountains.*	ein Foto machen
		thirst	*Some people died of thirst there. That's why it's called Death Valley.*	Durst
		track	*There was a track through the mountains.*	Weg, Pfad
		unbelievable	*That was an unbelievable adventure.*	unglaublich
■	6	**go for a walk**	*I went for a walk on a winter's day.*	spazieren gehen
		pray	*People usually pray in church.*	beten
		preacher	*Preacher is an American word for priest.*	Geistliche/r, Pfarrer/in
★	7	**print**	*You can see hand-prints of the stars in the pavement.*	Abdruck

UNIT 12 Survival

Revision Vocabulary

■ 1 **Complete the dialogue with the words in the box.**

dry
signal
spot
backpack
dirt

A Where are you going?
B I'm going mountain biking.
A And why have you got a [1]................................ on your back?
B My food's in there – it stays [2]................................ if it rains.
A Are you going to cycle on [3]................................ roads?
B That's right. And I'm going to see if I can [4]........................... some birds, too – I like bird-watching.
A Me, too. If you see an interesting bird, call me.
B OK, I'll try – but I don't know if there'll be a [5]................................ where I'm going.

Grammar Present perfect continuous

■ 2 **Complete the mini-dialogues with the phrases in the box.**

I've been telling
I've been running
I've been waiting
Have you been taking
have you been playing
I've been trying
has been helping
You've been saying
I've been teaching

1 **A** How long .... the guitar?
B For about two years.
A .... lessons?
B No – .... myself how to play.
A What? You mean, with no help at all?
B Well, my father .... me a little bit.

2 **A** I'm sorry I'm so late.
B You're very late! .... for almost thirty minutes. Why are you red in the face?
A .... – I tried to get here quickly.
B Oh. Well, have you got the tickets?
A No – I'm sorry again. There weren't any tickets left.
B What? Oh no! .... all my friends about this concert. And now, no tickets?
A Look, ... to get tickets for weeks – but it's impossible. Sorry.
B Please be quiet! .... sorry since you got here.

■ 3 **Complete the sentences so they are true for you.**

1 I've been learning English ....
2 My family has been living in our house/flat ....
3 I've been studying at this school ....
4 Our teacher has been helping us ....
5 I've been trying ....

END OF REVISION SECTION

■ **4** **Read the review of 'The Day After Tomorrow' in your Student's Book (p. 93) again. Tick T (*True*) or F (*False*).**

	T	F
1 The American government listens to the scientists.	☐	☐
2 Grapefruit falls on Tokyo.	☐	☐
3 Sam is trapped in a New York library.	☐	☐
4 Millions of Mexicans go to America.	☐	☐
5 Wolves chase Sam.	☐	☐
6 The dialogues are often not very good.	☐	☐

■ **5** **Use the words in the box to complete the sentences.**

earthquake
hit
flames
rescue
ran
erupted
trapped
travelled

1 The tsunami .... quickly towards the coast of India.
2 A boy was .... under a collapsed house.
3 A .... dog found the man after six days.
4 The coast was .... by a huge wave that was 10 metres high.
5 The .... that hit the island measured 6.9 on the Richter scale.
6 The volcano .... on May 16.
7 The wind blew the .... in the direction of the house.
8 When the flames came closer, people .... to their cars.

● **6** **Match the pictures and the sentences from 5.**

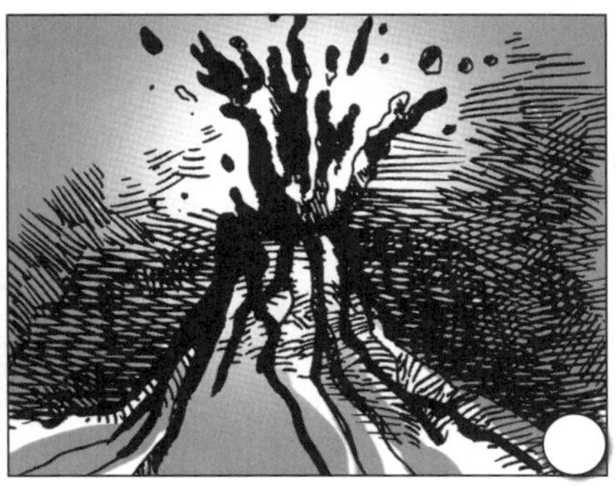

▶ SB pp. **93, 94**

7 Write *away* / *under* / *near* in each sentence.

1 Don't stand .... a tree if there's a storm.
2 Keep .... from a volcano if it's going to erupt.
3 During a tsunami, buildings .... the coast are in great danger.
4 If there's an earthquake, it's a good idea to lie .... a desk or table.
5 There was a mudslide .... the village.
6 During a flood, keep .... from electricity.

8 Read the text. Complete with the words in the box. There is one word you won't use.

collapsed
cracks
crushed
died
escaped
rescue
safe
earthquake

There was a terrible [1].. last night in Japan. It measured 7.2 on the Richter scale. Some streets in the cities have big [2].. in them. Many older houses [3].. and some people inside them were [4].. . Some people were lucky – they [5].. and now they are [6].. . Workers are trying to find people who are still alive and [7].. them.

9 Put the dialogue in the correct order.

- [ ] **B** Oh. Was it bad?
- [ ] **B** A thousand? That's awful. I'm sorry to hear that.
- [ ] **B** Earthquake? What earthquake?
- [1] **A** Did you read about the earthquake?
- [ ] **A** Yes, really bad. About a thousand people were killed.
- [ ] **A** The one in Indonesia. It happened last Friday.

10 Choose one of the sets of information. Write a dialogue like the one above.

FOREST FIRE
California • Last week • 400 houses destroyed

FLOOD
England • Yesterday • 12 people killed • 20 towns flooded

....
....
....
....
....
....

▶ SB p. 94

■ 11 **Read the text. Then answer the questions.**

Australian children in desert island disaster

Naseli and Lisa Nona were on their way in their boat from Badu Island to a birthday party on Thursday Island. With them were their four children, Stephen, 12, Norita, 10, Ellis, 15 and also their three-year-old brother Pete. The journey normally takes two hours and the family was about half the way between Badu and Thurday island when their boat's motor stopped.

Then the weather turned really bad and suddenly the boat was turned over by the heavy wind. The children and their parents stayed in the water near their boat for some time, but then Ellis, Norita and Stephen were told by their parents to swim to the nearest island. The three children swam for about three hours before they reached a little rock. They climbed onto the rock and hoped for a boat to come and rescue them. But nobody came and so the children had to stay on the rock for three days and nights without water and food. Then the sisters were told by Stephen to swim to another island. 'We must try to get there,' he said, 'or we'll die!'

The children were lucky. They were not attacked by any sharks and when they reached the island, they found plums and coconuts. Finally they were found on the island by their uncle after six days. Unfortunately, their parents and their little brother are still missing.

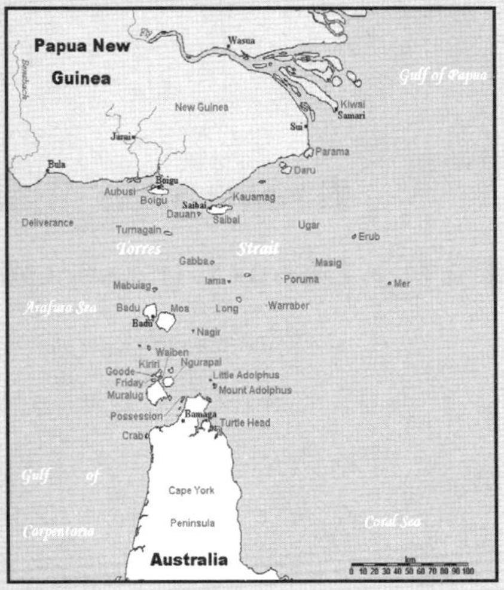

1 Why was the family going to Thursday Island?

....

2 Where was the family when their boat was hit by bad weather?

....

3 What other problem was there and what happened?

....

4 Why didn't the children stay with their parents?

....

5 Where did they stay for three days and why did they leave?

....

6 Who were the children found by?

....

7 How did they survive on the desert island?

....

8 How long did they stay on the second island?

....

■ 12 **Read the story 'Castaway' on p. 96 of your Student's Book again. Answer the questions.**

1 Why did the plane Chuck was travelling in crash?

....

2 What did Chuck eat and drink on the desert island?

....

3 What did Chuck use to draw a face on the ball?

....

4 How long did Chuck stay on the island?

....

5 What happened to Wilson?

....

6 How was Chuck saved?

....

▶ SB pp. **95, 97**

■ **13 Imagine you are going to stay on a desert island for a month. Write what you want to take with you.**

First of all I want to take a book with me. The book I'd take is ....
because ....

I love music and that is why I'd take ....

★ **14 Write down a few tips on how to survive holidays at home. Try to make them funny.**

....
....
....
....
....

Grammar Passive

■ **15 Decide if the sentences are passive or active.**

	Active	Passive
1 The hurricane destroyed thousands of homes.	☐	☐
2 Breakfast is cooked by the chef.	☐	☐
3 He was paid a lot of money for the photo.	☐	☐
4 We're not very happy with our room.	☐	☐
5 The teacher was 10 minutes late for the lesson.	☐	☐
6 The plane was full of people.	☐	☐

■ **16 Complete the text with the correct form of the verbs in the present simple passive.**

How a new MEGASTAR ...is found...! (find)

Read this leaflet carefully – you could be the megastar of tomorrow!

Fill out this card and send it to us. Tell us why you think you could be a superstar.

All the cards [1].. by our jury*. (read)
25 young people [2].. . (chose)
They [3]... to our studio. (invite)
They [4].. to sing their favourite song in front of a camera. (ask)
Their performance [5]........................... . (film) Then the films are [6]........................... by the members of our jury. (analyse)

It's that easy. Send in this card – and you could be one of the 7 MEGASTAR CANDIDATES.
A week later, each of these 7 young people [7]................. .... (ask) to sing 3 songs in front of a lot of people. Then the winner [8].. by these people – and the winner could be YOU! (choose)

VOCABULARY
***jury** – Preisrichter

▶ SB pp. 96, 97, 99

■ **17** **Write sentences for the pictures.**

1 worm / eat / bird
The worm was eaten by the bird.

2 boy / hit / football
....

3 race / win / a girl
....

4 dinner / make / dad
....

5 house / destroy / earthquake
....

6 boys / chase / dog
....

7 plane / delay* / fog
....

8 glass / break / cat
....

VOCABULARY: *delay – aufhalten

Everyday English The phone call

Look at the phrases on p. 98 in your Student's Book again. Use them to complete the dialogues.

1 **A** I think I need to buy a new mobile.
B .... But if I were you, I'd just buy a new battery.

2 **A** I think it's going to rain. Can I borrow your umbrella, please?
....
B Sure! ....
A Thanks.

3 **A** Somebody told Chris that I took Lisa to the cinema yesterday!
B Hey! .... I didn't tell him.

Word File

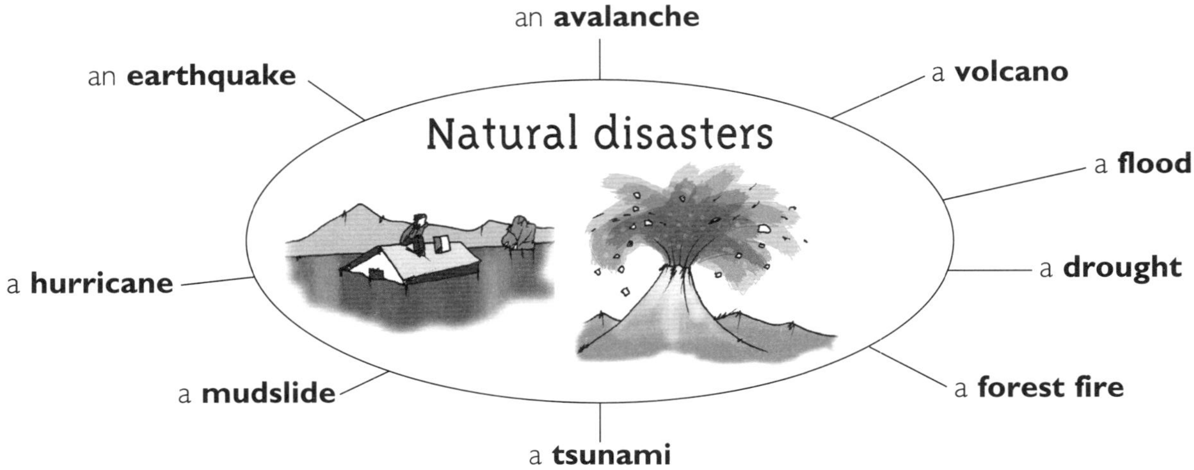

MORE Words and Phrases

■	2	**change**	*This could start a catastrophic change in the world's weather.*	Veränderung, Wechsel
		damage	*The houses were badly damaged.*	Schaden; (be)schädigen
		effect	*The film has amazing special effects.*	Auswirkung, Folge; hier: Effekt
		global warming (no pl)	*Global warming can change the world's weather.*	Erwärmung der Erdatmosphäre
		hailstone	*Hailstones can be as big as tennis balls.*	Hagelkorn
★	4	ash	*The volcano sent ash and rocks into the air.*	Asche
		disaster	*A great disaster of the modern world was the tsunami in 2004.*	Katastrophe, Unglück
		erupt	*The volcano erupted on June 3rd.*	ausbrechen
		evacuate	*60,000 people were evacuated from the island.*	evakuieren, räumen
		luckily	*Luckily, the evacuation saved thousands of lives.*	glücklicherweise
		measure	*The earthquake measured 6.6 on the Richter scale.*	(ab)messen
		survivor	*After the rescue operation only a few survivors were found.*	Überlebende/r
		warn	*Scientists warned about the danger.*	warnen
■	6	**injured**	*Many people were injured.*	verletzt
■	7	crush	*The car had been crushed under a tree.*	zusammendrücken; zerquetschen
●	8	castaway	*After the crash Chuck was a castaway on the island.*	Schiffbrüchige/r
		miracle	*Some time later, a miracle happened.*	Wunder
		raft	*Chuck built a raft to escape from the island.*	Floß
		wreckage (no pl)	*Plane wreckage was washed ashore.*	Wrackteile, Trümmer
★	10	**choice**	*You can choose a record or a book. It's your choice.*	Wahl
		desert **island**	*How do you survive when you are a castaway on a desert island?*	einsame Insel
		pleasure (no pl)	*It's a pleasure to be here.*	Freude, Vergnügen
★	11	**advice**	*I don't know what to do. Can you give me some advice?*	Rat
★	13	crack	*The windows and the walls of the building cracked in the earthquake.*	(zer)brechen, zerspringen

UNIT 13 Dilemmas

Revision Vocabulary

1 Add the vowels* to complete the 'disaster' words. Then match the words to the 'definitions'.

VOCABULARY
***vowels** – Selbstlaute

1 __ __ r t h q __ __ k __
2 __ v __ l __ n c h __
3 v __ l c __ n __
4 f l __ __ d
5 d r __ __ g h t
6 t s __ n __ m __
7 f __ r __ s t f __ r __
8 h __ r r __ c __ n __

☐ lots of trees are burnt
☐ river water goes into the streets
☐ a very, very strong wind
☐ not enough water
☐ lots of snow goes down the mountain
☐ when the ground shakes
☐ a huge wave that is started by an earthquake
☐ a mountain that has fire inside

Grammar Passive

2 Complete the sentences with words from the box. Match them with the pictures.

are taken
is connected*
can be sent
is put
are downloaded
are put

How digital cameras work

1 First a memory card .... in the camera.
2 Then the pictures ....
3 The camera .... to a computer.
4 The photos .... onto the computer.
5 Finally the photos .... into files.
6 Now they .... to other people in an email.

VOCABULARY
***connected** – verbunden mit

3 Choose a verb from the box and write it in the *past simple passive* to complete each sentence.

direct
discover
hold
invent
kill
paint
win
write

1 Wimbledon .... by Roger Federer from 2003 to 2007.
2 The film *Titanic* .... by James Cameron.
3 The internet .... by Tim Berners-Lee.
4 America .... by Christopher Columbus.
5 More than 200,000 people .... by the 2004 tsunami.
6 The 2008 Olympic Games .... in Beijing.
7 *Romeo and Juliet* .... by William Shakespeare.
8 *The Mona Lisa* .... by Leonardo da Vinci.

END OF REVISION SECTION

● **4 Find eight words in the wordsnake.**

picksnerdgroupcheekygroundeddetentionweirddilemma

■ **5 Complete each sentence with one of the words from 4.**

1 My parents got angry with me and they've .... me for a week!
2 He often gets into trouble for saying .... things to the teacher.
3 I don't know what the right thing to do is. It's a real .... for me.
4 He shouldn't wear those silly glasses – he looks like a .... with them.
5 If you talk in class, you'll get ....
6 He's a real bully* – he always .... on smaller kids.
7 Look at his clothes! They're all green! That's really .... !
8 I'm going out on Friday with a .... of kids from school.

VOCABULARY
***bully** – jemand, der andere tyrannisiert

■ **6 Put the dialogue in the correct order.**

- [ ] **B** What's the problem with being tired?
- [ ] **B** Well, if you studied more, you'd get better marks.
- [8] **B** Oh dear. My head hurts!
- [ ] **B** And if you slept more, you wouldn't wake up in time for school.
- [1] **A** I'd like to get better marks at school.
- [ ] **A** That's right. And then I'd lose marks for being late.
- [ ] **A** Well, if I got tired, I'd need to sleep more.
- [ ] **A** Yeah, but if I studied more, I'd get tired in the evening.

■ **7 Look at the pictures. Write three more dialogues.**

1 lose your door key

2 see a famous person

3 see your teacher at the school disco

4 be headmaster of your school

1 **A** *What would you do if you lost your door key?*
B *I'd go to my friend's house.*
2 **A** ....
B ....
3 **A** ....
B ....
4 **A** ....
B ....

▶ SB p. 103

8 Read the dilemmas and match them with the pictures.

Dilemma 1

Imagine your older brother asked you to give him an alibi for last night. He asked you to tell your parents he was with you. What would you do?

Dilemma 2

Imagine someone broke the classroom window when your teacher wasn't there. When she returned she asked you who it was. What would you do?

Dilemma 3

Imagine you were walking down the street and you found a wallet on the ground. What would you do?

9 Match the sentence halves.

Dilemma 1

1 If he asked me to give him an alibi,	☐ I wouldn't give him an alibi.
2 If he didn't tell me why he wanted one,	☐ I'd tell them.
3 If my parents asked me where he was,	☐ I'd give him one.

Dilemma 2

1 If I told the teacher,	☐ you'd probably all get detention, too.
2 If you didn't say anything,	☐ I'd say that I didn't know.
3 If the teacher asked me what happened,	☐ the other students would hate me.

Dilemma 3

1 If there was an ID card in the wallet,	☐ I'd keep it and leave the wallet.
2 If there wasn't an ID card in the wallet,	☐ I'd take it to the police station.
3 If I needed the money,	☐ I'd find the owner and give it back.

10 Write your answer for each of the three dilemmas. Choose sentences from 9 above, or write your own.

1 ....

....

2 ....

....

3 ....

....

▶ SB p. 104

11 **Read the story. Put the pictures in the correct order.**

A dilemma

I went to the cinema yesterday and I saw John outside – he's my best friend Sandra's boyfriend. I was talking to him and I could see that he was a bit nervous. I thought it was because Sandra hadn't turned up yet. (Sandra's always late.)

Anyway, suddenly this girl came over and she took John by the hand and said 'Come on, John, the film's going to start in a minute. I want to get some popcorn first.' And off they went. I was shocked and I decided not to watch the film – I just went home.

When I got home, the phone rang. It was Sandra. She asked me something about the maths homework. She was doing maths all evening. 'I couldn't go out,' she said. 'John was working for English and I had to do my maths homework.' I told her the answer to her maths problem and then I thought to myself: 'Should I tell her about John and that other girl?' I didn't know what to do and then Sandra just said 'Bye Jenny! Thanks for your help!' and she hung up. So in fact, I didn't have a chance to say anything to her.

The next day, after school, I was walking out of the school yard and I saw Sandra and John in the street. They were arguing like crazy! Shouting at each other, pointing fingers at each other, all that stuff. I was shocked – I just stopped and watched them.

Then Sandra saw me and she walked over to me. She was still really angry. 'You knew about this!' she shouted at me. 'You knew! You saw him at the cinema. Didn't you?' Then John came over and said 'Sandra, it's not Jenny's fault – shout at me, not at her!' But Sandra just looked at me and said: 'I hate you! I hate both of you!' And then she turned and walked away.

Since then, Sandra hasn't spoken to me, she hasn't phoned me, she doesn't even look at me. I don't see John either – he doesn't go to our school anyway. And so it seems I've lost two friends and I don't think I deserve it – I didn't do anything wrong.

12 **Read the story again and answer the questions.**

1 Why did Jenny think John was nervous outside the cinema?

....

2 What did Sandra ring Jenny about?

....

3 Why didn't Jenny tell Sandra about John and the other girl?

....

4 Where were Sandra and John when they were arguing?

....

5 Why was Sandra angry with Jenny?

....

6 Why does Jenny think she doesn't deserve to lose her friends?

....

▶ SB pp. 105, 106

13 Look and the pictures. What happened in the shop? What should the boy do? What would you do?

Grammar 2nd Conditional

14 Match the beginnings and endings of the sentences..

1 If I had enough money,	☐ you'd get better marks.
2 If my brother had a problem,	☐ I'd buy a new computer.
3 If I found some money in the street,	☐ would you tell me?
4 If you worked harder,	☐ I'd take it to the police station.
5 If I was president of Austria,	☐ I'd change lots of things.
6 If you knew the answer,	☐ I'd help him.

15 Put the verbs in brackets into the correct form.

1 If my father ......was...... (be) here, I ......would be...... (be) very happy.
2 If she .... (not live) in London, I .... (see) her more often.
3 If I .... (have) a dictionary, I .... (look) this word up.
4 If my computer .... (not be) broken, I .... (write) some emails.
5 If your mother .... (be) here, she .... (not let) you do that!
6 The teacher .... (be) angry if she .... (know).

16 Write the sentences.

1 I don't like Sally. I don't talk to her.
If I liked Sally, I'd talk to her. ....

2 He doesn't have a computer. I don't send him emails.
If ....

3 She's ill. She isn't at school.
If ....

4 I like you. I help you with your homework.
If ....

5 They're on holiday. They aren't here today.
If ....

6 My modem is broken. I don't surf the internet.
If ....

▶ SB p. 107

MORE Words and Phrases

		dilemma	*She's in a real dilemma.*	Dilemma, Zwangslage
★	1	cheeky	*Steve's really cheeky.*	frech, dreist
		be grounded	*Mom grounded me because I came home late.*	Hausarrest haben
		nerd	*He's not very popular with the other kids because he's a bit of a nerd.*	Streber, Outsider
		outsider	*Someone who doesn't have many friends and is alone.*	Außenstehende/r; Außenseiter/in
		pick on sb	*I don't like her. She picks on you all the time.*	auf jdm. herumhacken
		punish	*I'm going to punish you for not doing your homework.*	bestrafen
		punishment	*What do you think is the right punishment? No TV for a week?*	Bestrafung, Strafe
		rude	*You don't make friends when you are rude to other people.*	unhöflich
		stay behind	*He had to stay behind after school.*	zurückbleiben
★	2	I wasn't **born** yesterday.	*Don't think I don't know what you're talking about. I wasn't born yesterday!*	Ich bin nicht von gestern.
		by mistake	*I did the wrong homework by mistake.*	aus Versehen, versehentlich
		deserve	*Why do you think you deserve detention?*	verdienen
		detention	*Staying late after school as punishment.*	Nachsitzen
		It's his own fault.	*He is the one who did something wrong.*	Er ist selbst schuld.
		loser	*He's a bit of a loser.*	Verlierer/in
		mean	*Miss Bond is so mean and unfriendly.*	gemein, fies
		meet up	*Do you like meeting up with your friends?*	sich treffen
		not even	*She didn't want to talk to him. Not even in detention.*	(noch) nicht einmal
		poetry	*I like reading poetry.*	Dichtung, Lyrik
		serious	*I'm serious! I really do like poetry!*	ernst
		Serves you right.	*That serves him right.*	Das geschieht ihm recht.
		silent	*I won't say a word. I promise to be silent.*	still; ruhig
		be tired of sth	*I'm tired of warning you all the time.*	etwas satt haben
		trip	*Steve put out his leg and the nerd tripped.*	stolpern
★	3	**tell on somebody**	*Tina told on her friend.*	jdn. verpetzen
★	5	**get into trouble**	*It's no good getting into trouble with your parents, your parents, your teachers or your friends.*	Schwierigkeiten bekommen
■	7	ID (= identification)	*Do you have any ID with you?*	Ausweis
■	10	**ask sb out (for)**	*He asked his new girlfriend out on Saturday.*	jdn. einladen (auf)
		owe sb sth	*He owed his brother a lot of money.*	jdm. etwas schulden
★	12	loneliness (no pl)	*Loneliness is what you feel when you can`t talk to any of your friends.*	Einsamkeit
	Grammar	**get to know** sb	*She got to know his friends at the party.*	jdn. kennenlernen

EXTRA UNIT 14 Into the wilderness

Revision Vocabulary

1 Find eight words in the grid (→ ↓ ↗ ↘).

....

....

....

....

E	I	W	G	R	O	U	D	A	D
W	E	I	R	D	P	N	E	R	D
E	R	T	O	D	O	O	L	L	I
A	C	H	U	O	R	I	O	R	P
R	H	F	N	R	W	T	R	A	I
S	E	A	D	H	C	N	U	B	C
Y	K	E	E	H	C	E	D	B	K
A	K	Q	D	E	D	T	E	I	S
L	Y	U	R	E	I	E	A	O	A
A	M	M	E	L	I	D	E	R	T

2 Use the words in exercise 1 to complete the sentences.

1 **A** I'm going to make a pizza – ham and strawberry!
B You're .... !

2 **A** Wow! The teacher asked you lots of difficult questions today.
B I know. I always get the hard questions. I don't know why she .... on me!

3 **A** Jeremy only ever sits in front of his computer and writes programmes.
B Well, that's because he's a computer ....

4 **A** Why did the teacher send you out of the class?
B Well, the same thing as always. I was being .... to her.

5 **A** Did you invite a lot of people to your party?
B Yes, lots. All my friends from school and a .... of kids from my street.

6 **A** Come to the coffee shop with us after school.
B I can't – the teacher gave me ....

7 **A** What do you think? Shall we go to the cinema or stay home and do our homework?
B Oooh! What a .... ! What films are on?

8 **A** Dad – I'm really sorry, but I broke another glass.
B What? That's four glasses you've broken. OK, you're .... until Monday.

Grammar 2nd Conditional

3 Put the verbs in brackets into the correct form.

1 If we .... (live) in New York, I .... (watch) baseball all the time.

2 If she .... (like) me, she .... (talk) to me sometimes.

3 If I .... (have) games on my computer, I .... (not stop) playing them.

4 I .... (play) basketball if I .... (be) taller than I am.

5 If I .... (be) a teacher, I .... (not give) detention to any of the kids.

6 If you .... (can) travel anywhere in the world, where .... you .... ? (go)

7 They .... (not pick) on him if he .... (not be) so weird.

8 I .... (talk) to that bunch of boys if they .... (not be) such nerds.

END OF REVISION SECTION

■ **4** **Where have Mr and Ms Smith booked their holiday? Complete the puzzle and find out where they are going.**

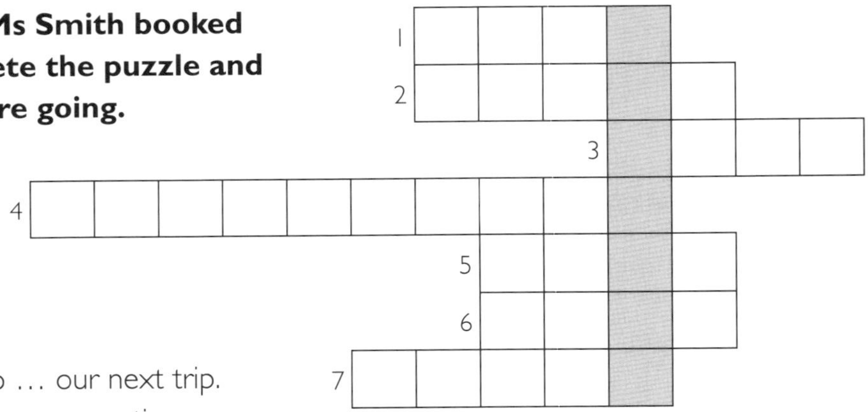

1 Tonight we're going to … our next trip.
2 We'll need to make a … reservation.
3 Let's find out … to do there.
4 We should buy a … to help with the language problems.
5 We're lost! Let's … at the map.
6 We're going to … a car when we're on holiday.
7 Let's … the area out on the web.

■ **5** **Read Oliver's email on p. 108 of your Student's Book again and decide if the sentences are true or false.**

	T	F
1 Oliver's going to school in Botswana.	☐	☐
2 People in Botswana don't have a lot of water.	☐	☐
3 Oliver found out about his holiday a week ago.	☐	☐
4 Oliver is excited about the trip.	☐	☐
5 His parents have already flown over to Botswana.	☐	☐
6 Oliver is flying next week.	☐	☐

■ **6** **Read the second text on p. 108 of your Student's Book and complete the fact file.**

FACT FILE

Botswana

Where is it? In ………………… Africa

How big is it? About ………………… times bigger than …………………

What's the population? …………………

Is it wild? Yes, it is. It's in the …………………

Does it have any problems? Yes, there's not enough …………………

What languages do people speak? English and …………………

What's the capital? …………………

▶ SB p. 111

■ **7** **Read the text about a tour to the Okavango Delta in Botswana.**

Classic Botswana

What is the Okavango Delta?

It is one of the world's most famous wilderness areas. The delta is formed by thousands of channels* of the Okavango River with clear water. There are lots of small islands and larger dry open areas with bush and lots of trees. The Okavango is home to more than 400 different kinds of birds and large herds* of buffalo, antelopes* and elephants. You will also find crocodiles, hippos, cheetahs*, leopards, lions and different kinds of monkeys.

What are the camps like?

There are camps with stone bungalows or very nice tents, each with a private shower and toilet. In each camp there is also a large dining room and a shop where you can buy souvenirs.

What can you do at the camp?

You get up at six o'clock and have a wonderful breakfast. Then at half past six the first drive of the day starts, and it ends at ten or eleven. When you stay in a camp in one of the large dry areas you will go on a game drive in a Landrover. When you stay in a water camp you will either go by boat or a canoe, which is called a mokoro. There are only seats for two people in a mokoro. The guide uses a long stick to push the canoe along.

When you come back to the camp lunch will be waiting for you. Then you can rest or relax until five. At five there is the second drive of the day and part of it will be in the dark. The guides will use a spotlight* to look for animals. When you come back at about nine, dinner will be waiting for you. After you may have a chat round the camp fire.
When you go to bed, a guide will go with you to your bungalow or tent as there may be wild animals such as elephants or lions around.

■ **8** **Choose and underline the correct options.**

1 You can see lots of big *cats / dogs* in the Delta.
2 There are *a few / lots of* types of monkeys there.
3 You *have to / don't have to* share toilets at the camp.
4 The morning drive starts at *six / half past six*.
5 The morning drive is about *five / seven* hours.
6 A mokoro travels *on water / on a road*.
7 The second drive is in the *morning / evening*.
8 You have dinner at about *seven / nine* o'clock.

VOCABULARY
***channels** – Kanäle
***herd** – Herde
***antelope** – Antelope
***cheetah** – Gepard
***spotlight** – Suchscheinwerfer

▶ SB p. 113

■ **9** **Choose the correct answers.**

A Have you [1].................................. your trip yet?

B Most of it. My dad's [2].................................. a car to drive us to the airport and we've [3].................................. the hotel reservation.

A What are you going to do there?

B I'm not sure. We haven't [4].................................. out about all the things there are to do.

A Why don't you [5].................................. out the area on the internet?

B That's not a bad idea. Maybe I can [6].................................. at a map of the area on-line.

A What about the language? Are you taking lessons?

B No. I think I'll [7].................................. a dictionary to use there.

A Well good luck, and don't forget to send me a postcard.

B I won't!

1	a) planned	b) found	c) looked
2	a) checked	b) hired	c) made
3	a) done	b) made	c) had
4	a) found	b) looked	c) asked
5	a) look	b) surf	c) check
6	a) buy	b) watch	c) look
7	a) buy	b) hire	c) make

■ **10** **Put the dialogue in order.**

☐ **B** We're not staying at a hotel. We're going camping.
☐ **B** A tent? Oh no. I forgot!
☐ **B** Yes – everything's ready!
☐ **B** No, it isn't. Perhaps I should make a list.

☐ **A** Great! Have you made a hotel reservation?
☐ **A** So, everything isn't ready, is it?
☐ **A** I think a list is a very good idea.
[1] **A** Have you planned your trip?
☐ **A** Camping? That's nice. Have you bought a tent?

■ **11** **Read the email. Then use the information to write a dialogue like the one in 10.**

Hi Jamie –
We've planned our holiday – I think. We're going to drive around England and visit lots of places. We aren't going camping this year, so we haven't bought a tent – we're staying in hotels. Dad has made all the reservations. Just a minute – I don't think he has hired the car yet! I think I should tell him, don't you?
Best Pauline

★ **12** **Look at the picture and then write a short story in your exercise books: "The 'Never-Again' Holiday."**

Grammar going to

■ **13** **Write what they are going to do in 10 years.**

....
....
....
....

■ **14** **Write the questions.**

1 **A** *What are you going to do at the weekend* ?
B I'm going to do nothing!

2 **A** What .... for the holidays?
B I'm going to stay home for three weeks.

3 **A** Who .... organise the party?
B My friends are going to help me.

4 **A** Why .... football today?
B Because my leg hurts.

5 **A** What .... when you leave school?
B I'm going to work in a bank.

Everyday English Red kite alert

Look at the phrases on p. 114 in your Student's Book again. Use them to complete the dialogues.

1 **A** Let's ask Mum if we can stay out late tonight.
B Why? She'll say No for sure. It's ....

2 **A** Hey you guys. Come with me to the cinema tonight.
B Sorry, no – we're all busy.
A Oh, all right. I'll go .... then.

3 **A** That new boy in class is awful. He's always talking and making trouble. .... I can't stand him!
B You're .... I don't like him either – no one does really.

MORE Words and Phrases

		wilderness	*Go into the heart of the wilderness.*	Wildnis
★	2	**check out** sth	*Check out were the capital is.*	etwas untersuchen, überprüfen
		dimwit	*Don't be a dimwit. Be clever!*	Dummkopf, Hohlkopf
		in case …	*I'll tell you again tomorrow in case you forget.*	für den Fall, dass…; falls
		official language	*The official language in Botswana is English.*	Amtssprache
●	3	**compare**	*You need to compare the size of the two countries.*	vergleichen
■	4	leopard	*A very fast wild cat.*	Leopard
		mine	*There are lots of diamond mines in Botswana.*	Mine (Ausgrabung)
		skin	*Selling leopard skin is illegal.*	Haut; hier: Fell
		wetland	*The Okavango is a large wetland.*	Sumpfgebiet
■	6	coral (no pl)	*I really like the coral necklace you have on.*	Koralle
		ivory (no pl)	*Some Africans illegaly sell ivory.*	Elfenbein
		otherwise	*We need to protect them. Otherwise they'll die out.*	andernfalls, sonst
		stuffed	*Animals are killed and then stuffed so people can keep them at home.*	ausgestopft
		tortoise shell	*Tourists buy thousands of tortoise shells every year.*	Schildkrötenpanzer
■	7	alarm clock	*An alarm clock will wake you up in the morning.*	Wecker
		at once	*If you see him, please tell me at once.*	sofort
		by the way	*By the way, I was glad I didn't have to drive.*	übrigens
		hyena	*Look at the hyena chasing the antelope.*	Hyäne
		impolite	*It's not nice to be impolite or rude to other people.*	unhöflich
		lodge	*Outside in the wilderness we lived in a lodge.*	Hütte; hier: Lager
■	9	bend	*We followed the car and came round a bend in the road.*	Kurve
		criminal	*The police arrested two criminals.*	Verbrecher/in
		engine	*Alex stopped the Land Rover and switched off the engine.*	Motor
		neither (of us)	*Neither of us said a word.*	keine/r (von beiden)
		ranger	*The ranger will show you around the park.*	Aufseher/in; Ranger/in
		slope	*The car went off the road and down a slope.*	Hang
		sunburn (no pl)	*Don't stay in the sun too long or you'll get a sunburn.*	Sonnenbrand
		turn over	*The car turned over and landed on its roof.*	(sich) umdrehen; hier: überschlagen

Meet the Standards

Next year you might have to take a test to check how good your English is ("Bildungsstandards").

MORE! helps you to prepare for the test.

Your test could be on one of the following areas:

Listening

Part 1: 10 short listening texts, each followed by one multiple choice question

Part 2: 2 longer listening texts, each followed by 5 multiple choice questions

Reading

Part 1: 10 short reading texts, each followed by one multiple choice question

Part 2: 2 longer reading texts, each followed by 5 multiple choice questions

Speaking

Part 1: Taking part in a conversation

Part 2: Talking for a longer time

Writing

Part 1: Writing a shorter text

Part 2: Writing a longer text

Meet the Standards

Listening

Next year you might have to take a test to check how good your English is. ("Bildungsstandards"). MORE helps you prepare for the test.

Tips:

- First, read the questions carefully. You are going to hear each text twice.
- When you listen for the first time, try to get a general idea of what it is about.
- The second time, concentrate on the questions and all the answers on the test sheet. Listen carefully and try to find out which answer is correct.
- Remember there is only one correct answer per question.
- When you are not absolutely sure, choose the answer that you think is most probably correct.
- If you don't understand every word, keep cool – try to understand as much as possible.
- Your listening test will consist of:
  - 10 short listening texts, each followed by 1 question
  - 2 longer listening texts, each followed by 5 questions.

The following practice test gives you 5 examples of short listening texts and 1 example of a longer listening text.
N.B.: the <u>real</u> listening test will be double the length of this practice test.

Part 1

Listen to texts 01 – 05 and answer the questions. You must give your answers on the ANSWER SHEET. Put a tick ✓ in the correct place on the ANSWER SHEET (p. 104).

01 Listen and say which sentence is wrong.

A The Tower of London was a prison a long time ago.
B The Beefeaters guard the Crown Jewels.
C The Beefeaters are all men.
D The Beefeaters' uniform is red and dark blue.

02 What's Ben's problem?

A The guitarist in his band is ill and they haven't got another one.
B Jonathan can't play on Saturday because his mum is ill.
C Ben is ill.
D The girl wants to play in his band.

03 The girl thinks that

A doing sports during the holidays is fun.
B a person should be active during the holidays.
C a holiday is for relaxing.
D doing nothing during the holidays is bad.

04 What message does Rod leave on Stuart's answer phone?

A He wants to invite Stuart to a football match.
B He wants to invite Stuart to a basketball match.
C He wants to tell Stuart that he is late for the basketball match.
D He wants to tell Stuart that he couldn't get tickets.

05 The man

A wants to go to Glasgow on the next train and buys a return ticket.
B wants to go to Glasgow on the train at 8.30 and buys a return ticket.
C wants to buy a return ticket to Glasgow for the next day.
D hasn't got enough money for the train ticket.

Part 2 (longer text)

You are going to hear a story about a man and a bear. Listen carefully and tick the correct answers. There is only one correct answer to each question.

06 The text is about

A a holiday in Canada.
B bears in Canada.
C a man who met a bear when he went running.
D keeping fit through running.

07 As he ran along the road the man

A became very tired.
B was having great fun.
C was having no fun because there was so much traffic.
D had a strange feeling.

08 When the bear came closer, the man

A was really worried.
B lay down on the ground.
C started shouting for help.
D ran away.

09 In the end the bear

A attacked the man.
B ran off because the man made so much noise.
C ran after the man for a short time and then disappeared.
D ran off because a car was coming.

10 After meeting the bear the man

A phoned his wife and she picked him up.
B ran back home.
C got a lift back home.
D hid in the woods.

Reading

Tips:

- Carefully read the text first.
- It is usually not important to understand every word in the text. Keep a cool head and try to understand as much as possible. When reading for the first time, try to get a general idea of what the text is all about.
- Then read the questions.
- Read the text a second time and look at the questions one by one. Try to find the exact place in the text that allows you to answer each question.
- Remember there is only one correct answer. When you are not absolutely sure, choose the answer that you think is most probably correct.
- Your reading test will consist of:
  - 10 short texts, each followed by 1 question
  - 2 longer texts, each followed by 5 questions.

The following practice test gives you 5 examples of short texts and 1 example of a longer text. N.B: the real reading test will be double the length of this practice test.

Part 1

Read Texts 01 – 05 and answer the questions below each text. You must give your answers on the ANSWER SHEET. Put a tick ✓ in the correct place on the ANSWER SHEET (p. 104).

My boyfriend can't dance. He thinks he can, but he's really, really bad. In the beginning I thought, "Leave him alone because he is enjoying himself when we dance. But then it got worse. How do I tell him? I don't want to make him sad. I care a lot about him, but ...

---

01 What's the best title for this text?

A My boyfriend loves parties.
B A girl with a problem.
C Going to a party.
D I can dance.

No dogs in playground

---

02 Where could you see this notice? Tick the correct answer.

A In a restaurant.
B In a park.
C In a football stadium.
D In a shop.

Well, they say that everything is big in Texas, but we are going to try to keep the text short. Austin is great for live music. They say you can always find someone playing day or night, weekday or weekend. And it's true.

Our next stop was San Antonio to see the Alamo. San Antonio is really hot, but the Alamo is worth the 2 hour trip from Austin. The Alamo is the place where Davie Crockett and two hundred Texans fought against 7,000 Mexicans. Imagine that!

03 This text is from

A a course book for geography.
B an advertisement.
C a travel blog on the internet
D a letter written by Davie Crockett.

Little Joe says to his friend Tim, "Guess how many golf balls I have in my pocket."
Tim says, "If I get it right, will you give me one golf ball?"
Little Joe says, "If you get it right, I'll give you both of them!"

04 What's the joke about?

A Little Joe has got no golf balls in his pocket.
B Little Joe has got one golf ball in his pocket.
C Little Joe has got two golf balls in his pocket.
D Little Joe has got more than two golf balls in his pocket.

There was a nature programme on. Richard was very quiet. He didn't answer his sister's questions, he just said "yes" or "no". Richard usually talked a lot when they were watching nature programmes. So Rachel said to him, "Are you having problems at school?" Richard didn't answer. He just got up from the sofa and left the room.

05 Which would be the correct first sentence for the text.

A Richard liked nature programmes.
B Richard had problems at school.
C Richard's sister Rachel was fifteen.
D Richard and his sister Rachel were watching TV.

Part 2 (longer text)

You are going to read two statements from teenagers about school uniforms. Read carefully and tick the correct answers below. There is only one correct answer to each question.

I think school uniforms are a good thing for several reasons. First of all, wearing a uniform makes you feel like you belong to your school. Other children in the town see your uniform and they immediately know which school you go to. You feel proud of *your* school. And then school uniforms make sure that all children are equal when they are at school. It means that children from poorer families look the same as those from richer families. Finally, from a personal point of view, I like wearing a school uniform for one simple reason: it means I don't have to worry what I'm going to put on every morning when I get up. The school has already decided for me.

Sally 3C

I think school uniforms should be stopped. I think they are a terrible idea. Let me explain why. I know some people say that uniforms are good because you can proudly show the world which school you go to. Well this is certainly not true where I live. School uniforms are one of the biggest reasons for fights between kids from different schools. Wearing the wrong colours in the wrong area of town can get you into big trouble. If we didn't have to wear a uniform, no-one would know which school you were from. But the biggest reason why I'm so against school uniforms is that they are ugly. I love clothes and I'd like to wear the clothes that I like at school. Clothes tell others who you are. Wearing the clothes I like would tell the others who I am.

James 3C

06 What is the best title for the text?

A Students don't like school uniforms.
B Students love school uniforms.
C What students think about school uniforms.
D School uniforms are ugly.

07 What does the text do?

A It tells us about British school uniforms.
B It tells us what two students think about school uniforms.
C It tells us why British students wear school uniforms.
D It tells us what a boy and a girl like.

08 Sally gives

- **A** one reason why she thinks school uniforms are a good thing.
- **B** two reasons why she thinks school uniforms are a good thing.
- **C** three reasons why she thinks school uniforms are a good thing.
- **D** more than three reasons why she thinks school uniforms are a good thing.

09 Sally thinks

- **A** it's a good thing when all students wear the same clothes at school.
- **B** it's not a good thing when all students wear the same clothes at school.
- **C** that students from poor families are not happy with school uniforms.
- **D** that students from rich families are not happy to wear school uniforms.

10 Sally says she likes wearing a school uniform because

- **A** she likes the colour of her uniform.
- **B** she needn't think what to wear every morning.
- **C** her friends like school uniforms too.
- **D** she looks good in it.

11 James gives

- **A** one reason why he thinks school uniforms are a bad thing.
- **B** two reasons why he thinks school uniforms are a bad thing.
- **C** three reasons why he thinks school uniforms are a bad thing.
- **D** more than three reasons why he thinks school uniforms are a bad thing.

12 James says

- **A** that it is a good thing that other people know which school you are from.
- **B** that school uniforms can get you into trouble.
- **C** that his school uniform is the wrong colour.
- **D** that parents think school uniforms are ok.

Speaking

Taking part in a conversation

Tips:

- Read your prompt card carefully. Underline the most important information.
- Think what you want to say. Make notes. Don't write full sentences, but key words.
- When you talk, look at the other person. Be friendly.
- When the other person says something, listen carefully. You can use phrases such as:

OK. So you're saying that …
I see what you mean, but …
I don't know for sure, but perhaps …
Let me think a moment. I think it would be good to …
Maybe we can …
It would be a good idea to …

Test Practice Activity 1

Work with a partner. Imagine you are friends. It's Friday evening. Student A makes a telephone call to student B.

Student A – you have had a very difficult week with a lot of work for school. You want to go on a bike ride on Saturday and go to the cinema in the evening.

Student B – you would like to listen to some new CDs on Saturday. In the evening, you would like to watch a DVD at home.

Study your prompt cards for 2 minutes. If you like, make notes. Then talk as much as possible. Make sure you both get a chance to talk.

PROMPT CARD A

In the phone call

- tell your friend why you have not had any time to meet him/her or talk to him/her.
- tell your friend what you did during the week and what was so difficult.
- ask your friend about his/her plans for the weekend.
- invite your friend to go for a bike ride on Saturday.
- make a suggestion to go to the cinema together on Saturday evening.
- suggest a film and say why you would like to see that film.

PROMPT CARD B

In the phone call

- tell your friend that you are sorry that he/she had such a lot of work to do.
- tell your friend what your plans for the weekend are.
- say why you are not very happy about a bike ride.
- say why it would be better to listen to CDs.
- give reasons why you do not want to go to the cinema
- say why you'd prefer to watch a DVD at home

Talking for a longer time

Tips:

- Read your prompt card carefully. Underline the most important information.
- Take about 2 minutes to think carefully about what you want to say.
- Make notes on a piece of paper. Write your ideas down in key words.
- Use phrases such as the following to make your talk flow better:

  First of all I'd like to say that …
  It's not so easy for me to say … because …
  When I think of … I think of …
  I'd love to see / visit … because …
  Another important point is …
  I almost forgot to say that …
  I think if I could choose, I'd …

- Talk for about 2 minutes.

Test Practice Activity

PROMPT CARD

Look at the pictures and talk about visiting a big city as a tourist.

Which city would you like to visit?
What do you know about it?
Why would you like to visit it?
Which of the places in the pictures would you find interesting?
Why? Why not?

Writing

PART 1 Writing a shorter text (40-60 words)

Tips:

- Carefully read the task. What is it exactly you have to write about?
- Make a little mindmap for your ideas.
- Organise your ideas.
- Then write your text. Keep the writing flowing.
- When you have finished, take a deep breath. Then slowly go through your text again.
- Ask yourself:
  - Did I write what I had to write about?
  - Are there any of my "favourite mistakes" in the text?
  - Have I spelt everything correctly?
- Correct your text.
- If there is time, pause a little and read though it again before you hand it in.

Test Practice Activity 1

Read the e-mail and write an answer to it. Make sure you reply to all the questions. Your text should be about 50 words. You have 8 minutes to write your text.

Hi Dave,

Sorry, but it's raining so much and I can't meet you at five o'clock. I planned to go to the café by bike, but not in this rain!!! Could you come to my place? Your dad could drive you here, couldn't he? Or shall we meet tomorrow? We must hand in the project by Friday, so there is still plenty of time.

xxx
Liz

PART 2 Writing a longer text

Test Practice Activity 2

Look at the picture and write a text of 120-150 words about one of the girls. Think of her name, country, family, hobbies, plans for the future, wishes and fears.

Answer sheet

Listening

Part 1

Tick ✓ the correct answer.

	01	02	03	04	05
A					
B					
C					
D					

Part 2

Tick ✓ the correct answer.

	06	07	08	09	10
A					
B					
C					
D					

Reading

Part 1

Tick ✓ the correct answer.

	01	02	03	04	05
A					
B					
C					
D					

Part 2

Tick ✓ the correct answer.

	06	07	08	09	10	11	12
A							
B							
C							
D							

Writing

Test Practice Activity 1

....

....

....

....

Test Practice Activity 2

....

....

....

....

....

....

....

....

....

....

....